CAN **YOU** READ THIS OLD WRITING?

Appoynt the mrs of Spittall's Hospital to give to Alexander Jack, taylor, ane infirme tradesman, whose wife whose his principall support is now rendered lame by a fatall accident, twelve pound Scotts for his and his families present necessity till Candlessmess next that the accounts be made: and recomends him to his own trade and the kirk session for farder supplie.

This page shows you what a typical old historical document can look like. This page of old writing was made nearly three hundred years ago. It comes from the records of Stirling's town council of that time. It's not easy to read, is it? Nowadays these old books are kept safely at the Archives department of Stirling council. People can still ask to look at them. Some of these old records were studied and used to write this book for you.

If you look carefully at the photocopied written page, you will see that one section near the bottom has been made lighter. The lighter part has been typed out to help you understand what the old handwriting says. This section is all about a tailor called Alexander Jack, who was allowed to live in Spittal's Hospital because he was very poor and his wife was injured in an accident. On page 34 you can read about the *hospital* which Robert Spittal founded.

Discover Old Stirling

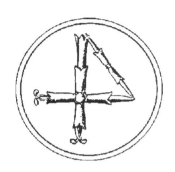

Craig Mair

With line drawings by Andrea Peters

Libraries
Community Services

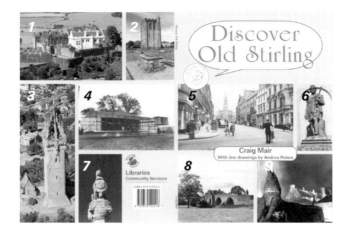

Cover Illustrations:

1 *Stirling Castle.*
2 *Cambuskenneth Abbey.*
3 *Wallace Monument.*
4 *Bi-plane built by the Barnwell Brothers.*
5 *King Street.*
6 *William Wallace, the steeple King Street.*
7 *Stirling Market Cross, Broad Street.*
8 *Old Stirling Bridge.*
9 *Burning of the wolf, Stirling Millennium celebrations.*

ISBN: 1 870 54241 X
© Stirling Council Libraries 2000

Acknowledgements and sources.

All photographs and engravings are from the Libraries' own collections unless otherwise mentioned below:

J. Brown:	Chapter 11
R. Chambers:	Chapters 12, 26
Corpus Christi College, Cambridge:	Chapter 2
Craig Mair:	Chapters 18, 20, 35
Andrea Peters:	Chapters 5, 6, 8, 14, 21, 22, 31, 36 and 'talking heads'
J. Proudfoot:	Chapter 3
E. Stair-Kerr:	Chapter 10
J. Fleming:	Chapter 15

Stirling Council Archives (Courtesy of the Keeper of the Records of Scotland):
Documents on back and front fly-leaves
Stirling Council Communications Unit: Chapters 1, 4, 7 and photographs on cover

This book is for Graeme

 Stirling Council Libraries gratefully acknowledge the financial assistance from the Guildry of Stirling, which has helped with publication costs.
The logo of the 'reversed four' has been used by the merchants of Stirling for several hundred years.

Contents

Stirling's town wall, built in 1547 to protect the town from English troops.

Steam-driven lorries disappeared from the streets many years ago. The iron-rimmed wheels must have made travelling in them very uncomfortable.

From 1874 horse-drawn trams ran between Bridge of Allan and Stirling, later carrying on to St Ninians.

Introduction

Welcome to the history of Stirling! It's a place full of people and stories from the past, and this book tells you about some of them.

But hold on there! How do we know what happened long ago? How did I find out what to write in this book? How do we *really* know? After all, you and I were probably not there at the time—even an older adult like me was certainly not at the Battle of Bannockburn, for example! So how can you be *sure* that the facts are true, and that this book isn't just a load of rubbish?

Well, finding out about Stirling's history is a bit like being a detective. You need clues to tell you what happened—*evidence* of the past. With these clues you can piece the story together. For example, you can find pictures and maps. Look at old buildings. Read about things in old newspapers. Find out from the letters and diaries people wrote long ago. Study old things in museums. Look at objects which people have found in the ground. Talk to old people. There are *loads* of ways! Stirling is absolutely full of clues—they're all around you, waiting for you to notice them.

In this book I have tried to tell you how we know about Stirling long ago. In every chapter you'll find the clues—the things which prove what happened. You can decide for yourself whether you believe me.

So here we go! In this modern new millennium you can find out about long ago. It's a great story, so happy reading!

Craig Mair

Courtyard of Argyll's Lodging.

Chapter 1

Meet your Ancestors

One day in the year 1819 (which is about 180 years ago) a workman was digging in a field near Airthrey Castle. He was making a trench in which to lay drain pipes. As he worked, his spade hit something unusual in the soil—a bone. But this was no ordinary animal bone. As he cleared the earth away, he found the entire skeleton of a large whale about 20 metres long.

Soon experts came to look at it. As they examined the creature, they found the remains of flint daggers and bone tools wedged among the bones. This whale, probably washed up or stranded on the shore about six thousand years ago, had been eaten by Stone Age people—our ancestors, the very first people to visit the Stirling area.

At that time the land looked very different from today. Forests grew on the hills, and down on the flat land beside the River Forth, where the houses of Braehead, Raploch, Riverside, Causewayhead, Cambuskenneth, Cornton and Bridge of Allan are today, there used to be a wide expanse of shallow seas and tidal marshlands. Perhaps that's how the whale got there.

Imagine a small group of Stone Age people— the very first ever to see the Ochil Hills or the silvery waters of the River Forth. Venturing cautiously into this uninhabited landscape, they came along the shores of the river from the direction of Falkirk. Here at Stirling was an area with plenty of food for the hunters to find. There were animals and berries in the forests, fish and shellfish in the river and plenty of wildlife in the marshes.

The first Stone Age explorers did not stay permanently in the Forth valley. When the local food supply was eaten they moved on, looking to camp and hunt in other places. But eventually, about five thousand years ago, people *did* begin to settle here. Some of their possessions, such as broken pottery bowls and flint tools, have been found all over the Stirling area. One man in the Raploch dug up a perfect stone axe-head in his back garden—it was four thousand years old! On the slopes of Dumyat you can still see the outline of fields where pre-historic settlers kept cattle and grew barley and wheat.

About four thousand years ago the first metal-workers began to settle in this area. They made bronze, which is a mixture of copper and tin. Quite a few of their bronze possessions, such as axes and arrow heads, have been found in the ground around Stirling. For example a battle-axe was found at St Ninians—who did it belong to, and how did it get there? We'll never know.

The Bronze Age people were mostly farmers. One of their farm houses was found near Plean. It was circular in shape, about seven metres across, and the roof used to be held up by wooden posts. You can still see the ditch which surrounded the houses for protection. Another farm lies under the present Police Headquarters at Randolphfield. It had a farmhouse and a separate building for the animals. What makes this example interesting is that it was first discovered by a 'dowser', who detected the buildings under the ground just by using sticks to point where they were.

The local Bronze Age people were also very interested in burials. When someone important died they placed the body in a stone coffin made with flat slabs, and then covered the whole box over with a huge pile of earth to make a little hill or *burial mound*. The 'Fairy Knowe' beside the second green on Bridge of Allan golf course is a good example. In 1868 it was opened by experts to see what was inside. They found some bones, a clay pot and six flint arrowheads.

For over two thousand years Bronze

Age people lived peacefully in the Forth valley. But then they were swept away by the Celts—fierce warriors with better iron weapons who came from the south to settle in the area. They belonged to many different tribes which sometimes attacked each other, so they built forts (called duns) to protect themselves. You can still see the remains of these defences, mostly ditches and walls, on hilltops all around Stirling, such as the Gowan Hill, beside the Wallace Monument, and at Castlelaw near Cambusbarron. One local tribe was called the Maeatae (pronounced *Ma-yet-eye*) and their fort was on the hill we now call Dumyat—the dun of the Maeatae.

In the year AD 80 the Romans invaded Scotland. They came to push back the wild Celtic tribes because they threatened southern Britain, so it was only soldiers who marched into the Stirling area. The defences of one of their forts can still be seen at Ardoch, next to the village of Braco, a few miles from Stirling. You can also see the remains of forts and the Antonine Wall in the area around Falkirk, but there's nothing much to see in Stirling. The marks of possible Roman ditch defences can still be seen at the back of the Smith Art Gallery and Museum and partly under the King's Knot—the best way to view them is from the walls of Stirling Castle. Otherwise, only a few Roman coins, perhaps dropped by careless soldiers, have been discovered.

So these are our ancestors—the first people to settle in the Stirling area, long before there was any town or castle.

Stirling and the River Forth.

LONG AGO STIRLING AND THE FORTH VALLEY WAS ALL **MARSHY** LAND WHERE HUNTERS LIVED.

Chapter 2

How the Town Began

When did the first houses appear at Stirling? The fact is that no-one knows. It is possible that the first settlement was at St Ninians, where there has been a church for hundreds of years. On the other hand, the castle hill is also an obvious place for a village or a fort—on dry land but surrounded by marshes and cliffs for protection. Some old papers, written about 1200 years ago, mention a settlement in the area called Urbs ludeu or Giudi—perhaps Stirling's original name!

For many years rival tribes fought for control of the Stirling area. For much of the time the Picts held the rock, but sometimes they were forced out by attacks from their enemies the Angles. Then the Scots (a tribe which moved to Scotland from Ireland around the year AD 500) also began to attack into the area. Later the Danes also tried to attack into the area from England. It was quite a battleground!

If you look at a picture of Stirling's old crest or coat of arms, you will see a wolf on it. This animal is always shown crouching on a rock. You can also see it on the badge of Stirling County rugby club. The wolf comes from a legend about old Stirling, when the area was ruled by the Angles.

One night, more than 1000 years ago, the enemy Danes were sneaking up to attack the town. The guard had fallen asleep and did not realise the danger, but he was woken by the howling of a wolf. He was just in time to call the others and the Danish attack was beaten—thanks to the wolf's warning. It is only a story, but it reminds us that there must have been some kind of village, and probably also a fort, at Stirling long before the present houses or even the ancient castle were built.

About the year AD 843 a very important battle was fought somewhere near Stirling. In this battle the Scots, led by their king Kenneth MacAlpin, defeated the Picts and finally became the rulers of most of what we now call Scotland. No-one knows exactly where the battle happened, but a big tall stone stands in a field near Stirling University's golf course. Some experts believe that it may mark where the battle was fought. From then on the Scots occupied the castle rock. It was such a strong place that Scottish kings probably lived there too, but this cannot be proved.

Somewhere between the years AD 1107 and AD 1115 King Alexander the First arranged to have a church built in his castle at Stirling. We know this because his letter still exists—imagine a letter nearly one thousand years old! It is the first definite evidence which *proves* that the castle was already there by that time. Unfortunately for the king, he didn't have long to use the new church because he died at Stirling Castle in AD 1124.

If there was a royal castle, there was almost certainly also a community nearby. Any king living there would have needed merchants to provide his food supplies and craftsmen to repair his castle. They would have lived in houses near the castle.

opposite: *This thirteenth century map shows Stirling Bridge, Strivelin Pons as the only link between southern Scotland and the north.*

LOOK HOW **SMALL** STIRLING USED TO BE.

The first picture of Stirling.

When King Alexander the First died, the next king was his younger brother David. He decided to make Stirling into an official 'royal burgh'. He gave the town a special paper called a charter, which listed the rights which the people were allowed to have. This probably happened in the year AD 1124, which means that Stirling is one of the four oldest royal burghs in Scotland. The other three are Edinburgh, Perth and Dunfermline, which were also made in the year 1124—that's almost 900 years ago!

King David's old charter does not exist any more. It probably said that the people of Stirling were allowed to have a weekly market (which was good, because folk would have come from all around to spend their money in the town). Probably the town was also allowed to have its own town council—people chosen by the inhabitants themselves, instead of a sheriff sent by the king. It is possible the king also said that the town could have a wall round it for protection. You would think that any town could do this, but this was not allowed unless the king gave special permission.

What did Stirling actually look like so long ago? Firstly, it was very small—only one or two streets where Broad Street is today. The houses were made of wood and clay, with straw roofs. Because of this, the town accidentally burned down several times. We know this because experts found the charred remains of some houses when they dug in the ground near Broad Street.

Close to the houses stood the town's first church, probably made of wood, but in the same place where the Church of the Holy Rood stands today.

So that's how Stirling started. Very different from today, isn't it?

Chapter 3

The Battle of Stirling Bridge

In the year 1296 the English invaded Scotland. The Scottish army was defeated and soon the whole country was conquered. The Scottish king, John Balliol, was captured and sent to the Tower of London. English soldiers garrisoned every castle and guarded every town. The country was completely beaten—or so it seemed.

Only a few brave Scots dared to struggle on against the English. Most Scottish people thought they had no chance. One of these freedom-fighters was William Wallace. His attacks on the English were so successful than eventually the English king sent an army to capture him. Wallace knew that the English soldiers would have to cross the River Forth at Stirling, where there was a wooden bridge. This bridge was about fifty metres up-river from the present old stone bridge at Cornton. We know this because experts have found the foundations of the bridge's legs, buried under silt in the river-bed.

At that time the flat valley of the River Forth was still very marshy. It got even worse, with big pools of water, every time the tide came in. From the wooden bridge, a narrow cart-track led across the marshlands to the dry rising ground where Airthrey is today. Because of the marshes, this road was built higher so that travellers would not get wet. This kind of road is known as a *causeway*, which is why the place where it ended is now called Causewayhead.

Although Wallace had help from Andrew of Moray and his highland fighters, the Scottish army was still quite small—perhaps about three or four thousand men. They were mostly poor folk and their weapons were just spears and swords. The English had a much bigger army—perhaps as many as 10,000 well-armed foot soldiers and bowmen, and around 300 armoured knights mounted on big heavy battle-horses. It did not look a very promising situation for the Scots!

Wallace and Moray had a plan, however. The wooden bridge was very narrow—probably only wide enough to let two horsemen cross side by side. The Scots would let some of the English cross over.

Then, as the enemy came along the narrow causeway, they would launch the attack, block off the bridge to stop any more English getting across, and defeat those trapped on the Cornton side. Did it work? Well, read on!

On the morning of 11th September in the year 1297, the English army began to file across the bridge. The smaller Scottish force stood patiently on the slopes of the hills at Causewayhead, waiting for the signal to attack. The first English troops to cross were knights on their heavy horses. They must have made a very impressive sight with their armour shining and banners flying. But crossing the narrow bridge took ages, and all the time the tide was coming in and the land was getting marshier.

The Battle of Stirling Bridge.

Local legend says that Wallace and Moray watched the English crossing from a viewpoint where the Wallace Monument is today. Certainly it's the best place from which to observe the flat land below. For several hours they watched the enemy knights cross the bridge and gather on the near side to come down the narrow causeway track two-by-two. And still the tide was rising.

When about half of the English army was across the signal was given to attack. Legend says that

Wallace blew a horn so that everyone could hear. With cheers and shouts the Scottish troops charged across the marshy lands towards the English. They didn't care if they got wet—most didn't wear armour anyway, so it didn't bother them.

What could the English knights do? They were on heavy horses. If they stepped off the narrow track they would sink into the boggy land. They were trapped unless they could get back across the bridge to safety. Unfortunately for them, they had no chance. Some Scots reached the end of the bridge and blocked it with their long spears. This stopped English reinforcements from getting to the battle, but also no-one could escape either.

Most of the English knights were killed, dragged from their horses by the Scots or drowned in the marshland and tidal pools. When the English on the other side of the river saw the slaughter, they ran away. Their bowmen could not fire in case they hit their own men. The spearmen were stuck on the wrong side of the river, unable to help. All they could do was save themselves. One of those who was killed was the hated English lord, Hugh of Cressingham. Legend says that Wallace had his skin cut off in strips—he is said to have used some of it to wrap round his own sword handle.

The battle of Stirling Bridge was a great victory for the Scots. For the first time in history, foot-soldiers had defeated mounted knights, even though experts had always said it was not possible. It made the Scots truly believe that they *could* beat the English and win back their freedom.

You can learn more about Sir William Wallace if you visit the Wallace Monument. One of the star attractions there is Wallace's sword—but beware! It has been repaired and had bits replaced so often that little, if any, of the original sword remains.

THE **WOODEN** BRIDGE WAS CLOSE TO WHERE THE OLD STONE ONE STANDS TODAY.

Chapter 4

The Battle of Bannockburn

By the year 1314 Wallace was dead, captured and executed by the English. Robert the Bruce was king of Scots and the war against England was still going on. Most of Scotland had been recaptured so things were going quite well. In June 1314, however, an enormous English army, led personally by King Edward the Second, crossed the border and advanced into Scotland. Their mission—to rescue Stirling Castle, the only important fortress in Scotland still occupied by English troops. For months the Scots had been besieging it. It had to be saved.

We don't know how many men this army had—probably between 20-30,000 men, mostly spearmen and bowmen, but with up to 5,000 mounted knights. Some reports say that, with all the baggage waggons, the whole force stretched for over twenty miles along the dusty summer road from England. Some size!

How was Bruce supposed to stop them? He seems to have had about 10,000 men—hardly enough to stop the much larger English army. He had done well so far because he had used hit-and-run tactics and had not fought the English in a proper battle. But this time he had no choice.

On the afternoon of 23rd June 1314, the first English knights came up the road from Larbert and, about where the Granada motorway service station is, had their first sight of the castle. There were only three or four miles to go. They must have felt very confident.

Ahead lay the Bannock Burn, then the road passed through a forest just beyond. Another track branched off to Stirling, but it crossed over marshy ground near the River Forth. As expected, the knights on their heavy battle horses stayed on the dry road and began to splash through the Bannock Burn towards the forest. This was just what Bruce wanted. He had dug deep holes called *pottis traps* in the road, camouflaged over but with spikes in them. He had also scattered pyramid-shaped pointed spikes called *caltrops* all over the grass. Soon the knights' horses began to stumble into the holes and panic began. Some horses stood on the caltrops and ran about in terrible agony with spikes in their hooves.

Just then a young English knight called Henry de Bohun recognised King Robert the Bruce and charged at him in a man-to-man combat. The story goes that Bruce was on a smaller horse, less impressive to look at but more manoeuvrable. As the two men rode towards each other de Bohun lowered his lance and urged his horse into a full gallop. Bruce had only a battle-axe. But at the last moment he ducked, swerved his horse out of the way and, as the big heavy horse thundered past, he rose in his stirrups and smashed his axe through the back of de Bohun's helmet into his head. The Scots were jubilant—first blood to them! A famous statue of King Robert now stands in the area where this incident happened.

The pottis traps and de Bohun's death caused most of the English army to hesitate, but Sir Robert de Clifford was more determined and led a group of three hundred fully armoured mounted knights on a charge towards the castle. Seeing the danger, Lord Randolph hurried with five hundred spearmen to block the road. Normally knights would easily have swept such puny opposition aside, but the Scots courageously stood firm and stopped the English from reaching the castle. No-one really knows where this brave event happened, but nowadays the police headquarters building is at a place called Randolphfield, while nearby is Clifford Road. Perhaps that's the area where it occurred.

By now it was late afternoon, so the English decided to camp overnight and finish the journey next day. Taking the side track, they headed down towards the marshlands of the River Forth. That night they slept in a good place, protected from a surprise attack by the Bannock Burn on one side, the Pelstream Burn on the other, and the pools of the River Forth behind them. Exactly where Bruce wanted them to be.

On the morning of 24th June 1314 the English awoke to find the Scots already lined up for battle

The statue of King Robert the Bruce at Bannockburn.

in front of them. What had been a safe campsite was now a marshy battlefield—unsuitable for heavy English horses, too narrow to use all their foot soldiers, and probably full of midges (imagine *them* inside your armour!). First the knights charged. Bruce had his men arranged in four huge circles called *schiltrons*, each with over 1000 men packed tightly into a group. When the knights attacked, they held out their long spears so that the horses could not get near them. So this idea failed.

Next, the English tried a different tactic. They ordered their bowmen to fire into the massed schiltrons. To begin with, they hit many Scotsmen but Bruce ordered his cavalry to attack. On lighter horses, they galloped over the marshy ground more easily and forced the bowmen to retreat.

Now the English spearmen were ordered to advance. But they could not spread out because of the Bannock Burn and most of them were behind the line of battle contact, uselessly shoving forward as they splashed through the pools and marshes of the Forth. For hours this struggle went on, but gradually it became clear that the English were slowly being driven backwards. Then King Edward was seen escaping from the battle, protected by a bodyguard of knights. You can imagine what the rest of the English army felt!

Just then, even more Scots began to charge onto the battlefield. They were the 'Sma' Folk'—the cooks and servants of the Scottish army who had been kept well away from the fighting. But they wanted to be part of the victory too! As they charged down from Coxet Hill (where Cultenhove is today), the English finally panicked and began to flee in all directions. Hundreds were killed as they tried to escape across the marshes. And so it ended—the greatest victory in Scottish history.

Cambuskenneth Abbey

Have you ever been to look at Cambuskenneth Abbey? It stands on the other side of the Forth from Riverside and you can get there by crossing a footbridge to the village of Cambuskenneth. You can also go by road from Causewayhead—take the direction to Alloa and turn right where a brown road sign points to the abbey.

There used to be lots of abbeys in Scotland but now there are only a few, though you can still see the ruins of some others. Cambuskenneth Abbey was begun by order of King David the First about the year AD 1140. At first it was known as the Abbey of St Mary of Stirling—that's why there is a St Mary's Wynd in Stirling. It used to be the road which led out of the town to the bridge, and from there to the abbey.

Cambuskenneth was one of the most important abbeys in Scotland. Kings such as Robert the Bruce sometimes visited the place. Sometimes the Scottish parliament met there. In the year 1488 King James the Third was murdered nearby at Bannockburn—his body was brought to Cambuskenneth Abbey for burial. You can still see his grave at one end of the church—did *you* know that a Scottish king lies buried in Stirling? In 1559, however, (by which time not many monks lived there anyway), the abbey was closed and most of the buildings were destroyed.

The place is deserted now, but Christian monks used to live there. The monks belonged to the Augustinian order and they wore brown robes.

There was a *dormitory* where they all slept in one big room, a *refectory* where they ate their meals together, the *chapter house* where they met each morning to plan the day's activities, and several other buildings such as the kitchen and the infirmary. The most important building was, of course, the enormous church where the monks went to sing and pray. They worshipped there eight times every day, starting at 2 o'clock each morning—imagine that!

There's not much to see nowadays. Apart from one tower in which the church bells used to hang, all the buildings are gone. After the abbey was closed, people came and took away the stones to build other places in the town—why waste money cutting new stones from a quarry, when you could help yourself to perfectly good stone blocks from the abandoned abbey buildings? Today you can still see the outline of some of the abbey's buildings, but the walls are only knee high. You have to read the explanatory notice boards to imagine what the abbey used to look like when the monks lived there.

STONES FROM THE ABBEY WERE **RE-USED** TO MAKE OTHER BUILDINGS IN OLD STIRLING.

Cambuskenneth Abbey.

Chapter 6

A Royal Tournament at the Castle

On 18th June 1449 a special ship docked at Leith harbour near Edinburgh. On board was a very important passenger—Princess Mary of Gueldres, from Burgundy in France. She had come to marry James the Second, the King of Scotland. Fifteen days later the ceremony was held at Holyrood Abbey in Edinburgh.

Later that summer the king held a great tournament at Stirling Castle. It was part of the celebrations for his recent marriage. The main contest was between three knights from Burgundy and three Scottish knights—each champions from their own countries. The tournament was held on the Haining, a field just below the cliffs and walls of the castle next to where the King's Knot is now. A special royal grandstand was built specially for the occasion. From here the king and queen and the various Scottish and Burgundian dignitaries could watch the fighting.

For days beforehand, knights and lords came to Stirling from all over Scotland, especially to attend the year's greatest tournament event. It is said that the entire area surrounding the King's Park became a sea of colourful tents and pavilions as Scotland's most important people arrived for the show. Stirling can rarely have been so crowded or so busy. It must have been a memorable time for local folk.

At last the day came. On the morning of the contest the six knights emerged from their tents in their armour. Each man was armed with a lance, a battle-axe, a sword and a dagger. It was to be a fight to the death, or until the king ordered the fighting to stop. Then with a blast of trumpets the six champions commenced battle.

First they charged each other on horseback but their lances soon split and were thrown away. Then they fought on foot in close combat. As at a boxing match, the crowd roared on its favourites, cheering each well-struck blow. Sometimes there were gasps as battle-axes or swords swung and clashed on steel armour. Sometimes men stumbled or were knocked down, but always they got to their feet and carried on. Mostly, however, the Scots were forced into desperate defence.

Eventually the king threw down his baton, as a signal to end the contest. It is said that people had to pull the struggling warriors apart, such was their eagerness to continue fighting for the honour of their countries. Though neither side could claim a clear victory, general opinion gave the French knights a win. For the assembled spectators it was a stirring occasion—something to talk about for many years.

The King was pleased with the day. It had been a great contest, fit to celebrate the royal marriage between Scotland and Burgundy. That evening he praised the courage and skills of each of the contestants at a feast in the castle. Later, when the foreign knights went home, they went off laden with gifts from the King of Scotland.

17

Chapter 7

Murder at Stirling Castle

Stirling Castle.

DID **YOU** KNOW THE CASTLE WAS THE SCENE OF A **MURDER**?

In the year 1452 Scotland's king, James the Second, committed murder, and as a result the town of Stirling was destroyed. Here is why, and how, it happened.

At that time the Scottish royal family was the Stewarts. But there were plenty of other people who wanted to become king instead—Scotland's kings had many enemies. One of the biggest threats to them was the Earl of Douglas, a powerful warlord descended from King Robert the Bruce whose castles were mostly in the south of Scotland. When the king heard that Douglas had made plans with other powerful families to have a rebellion against him, he called the earl to Stirling Castle to explain himself.

The Earl of Douglas was not stupid. He realised that it could easily be a trap and he refused to come to the castle. The king wrote a letter promising that Douglas would not be harmed and so, persuaded by this guarantee of safety, the earl duly turned up at the castle. It was February 22nd 1452.

Inside, the two men sat down to dinner. After eating, the king took Douglas aside into a small room. Here he told the earl that he knew about his plan and demanded that Douglas should stop this rebellious plotting—but the earl stubbornly refused. You must remember that both men had probably drunk some wine during their dinner. Remember too that the king was aged only twenty-two and Douglas was just twenty-seven—both violent, hot-headed, boastful young fighters.

The king was enraged by Douglas's refusal to be loyal to him. Almost certainly in a fit of anger and exasperation his temper boiled over. He pulled out his dagger and stabbed Douglas in the throat. Hearing the commotion, the king's guards came running to help and speared the wounded earl several more times until he was dead. Then, according to local tradition, they threw the body out of a small window into that part of Stirling Castle which is now called the Douglas Garden, where the corpse was hastily buried.

What could the Douglas family do to about this murder? The king was safe inside Stirling Castle, so they couldn't get him. Instead, a few weeks later, six hundred Douglas men came to Stirling town. Tying the king's worthless letter of safe conduct to the tail of a horse, they dragged it through the muddy streets. Then, having made their protest, they burned the town down and went away.

So that's how the town was destroyed by the Douglas family in revenge for a murder by the king.

Chapter 8

Stirling's Old Bridge

Just how old is Stirling's 'Auld Brig'? No one knows for sure, but it was probably built about the year AD 1500 during the time of King James the Fourth. Before then, people still used the remains of the old wooden bridge, where William Wallace fought the English in 1297. Old documents tell us that the wooden bridge was there at least as far back as the year 1214. It had been repaired many times, however, which is why it was eventually replaced by the stronger stone one which you can still see today.

At one time the road over the bridge was much steeper than today. It has been levelled out at least five times over the years, to make it easier for traffic to cross over. If you look carefully at the side walls of the bridge you can see where the previous levels used to be. To begin with there was also a large archway at each end. The arch at the Cornton end had strong gates to stop enemies from crossing the bridge and getting into the town. Later these arches were taken down and replaced by the pointed pillars which are still there today.

Anyone who crossed the bridge had to pay a *custom* or charge. Half-way over the bridge was a little booth where the *customar* collected the payments. You can still see the recess where he sat, although the roof which kept him dry is now gone. People also had to pay for any goods or animals which they had. Old records of the town tell us how much the charge was to cross over. In 1612, for example, the cost was two pennies for every horse load of goods, twelve pennies for each barrel of wine, eight pennies for every barrel of beer, two pennies for each load of flour, two pennies for each cow, and two pennies for every five sheep.

If you read Chapter 22 you will find out why the bridge was blown up in 1746. Until the bridge was repaired three years later, Stirling made no money from charging people when they crossed the bridge—it was a big loss for the town.

Have you ever wondered what kind of people must have crossed by that old bridge? Kings and queens, clan chiefs and generals, the poet Robert Burns and the writer Sir Walter Scott. But also lots of ordinary folk—soldiers with sore feet, cow herds bringing animals to market, country girls coming into Stirling to shop, wagonners bringing coal from Alloa, fishermen with salmon from the river, Cornton farmers with cheese and milk to sell. . . . The list is endless!

And so it went on until 1833, when the 'auld brig' was considered too narrow for stagecoaches and the present road bridge was built next to it.

I WONDER HOW MANY PEOPLE HAVE CROSSED THIS BRIDGE IN 500 YEARS?

Chapter 9

Damian the Flying Monk

One day, probably in the year 1507, a large crowd, headed by King James the Fourth himself, gathered on the ramparts of Stirling Castle and gazed out over the surrounding landscape. From the castle's position high on its hill they could see across the smoky huddled houses of nearby Stirling and the winding loops and flat marshlands of the River Forth to the mountains further off.

Almost certainly, however, one man in the crowd wasn't thinking about the view, for in the next few moments he was about to jump off the battlements and fly all the way to France—or so he said. He had even promised that he would arrive there before the King's ambassadors could reach Paris overland. This unlikely airman was John Damian, nowadays known as the 'Flying Monk' of Stirling. If he was looking out over the castle's walls at all, it was probably at the cliffs dropping vertically downwards from his vantage point, and he was doubtless thinking nervously that it was a very long way to fall! You've only got to look at the castle to see that for yourself.

So who was this Damian, and how did he come to be standing on the castle walls waiting for permission to take off? No-one really knows very mush about him. He was probably French or Italian and had wormed his way into the favour of King James the Fourth by claiming he knew the secrets of *alchemy* – the scientific skill of turning ordinary metals like lead into gold. Naturally the king was very interested! Hoping to become a rich man, he allowed Damian to do his experiments at the castle.

Old records from the royal treasury accounts show that the king made many payments for curious things like lumps of glass, saltpetre and coal for a furnace at Stirling during the years 1503 to 1508. These may have had something to do with Damian's experiments, but we will never know exactly what he was up to. Eventually it became clear, however, that it was all a waste of time and money. No gold appeared, and gradually the king lost patience with his foreign guest.

Damian had to find some new way to keep the king interested in his activities. That's why in 1507 he made the startling announcement that he would fly to France from the ramparts of Stirling Castle. And so it was that a large crowd gathered to watch the historic event. Feathered wings were strapped on to his arms and, with all preparations now complete, he stood on the battlements and took off.

We will never know if Damian really believed he would actually fly. However, with a frantic flapping of his wings he threw himself from the castle walls, seemed momentarily to float out for a couple of metres—and then plummeted straight down to earth more than 75 metres below. Luckily he fell into the castle's dungheap which gave him a soft, if smelly, landing. Amazingly, in spite of dropping the equivalent of about twenty-five storeys, he suffered nothing worse than a broken thighbone—and a lot of embarrassment.

Legend says that Damian even had an explanation for this failure. He claimed the problem was that he had used chicken feathers to make his wings. But everyone knows that hens are farmyard creatures which can't fly—he should have used eagles' feathers, he said. Then he would have soared away like the king of birds. Luckily for him, the king laughed.

So there you have it. The story of the first man ever to fly (well *nearly*!) in Scotland.

IMAGINE THINKING YOU COULD **FLY** WITH JUST CHICKEN FEATHERS!

Chapter 10

The King who Dressed in Disguise

HE DOESN'T LOOK MUCH LIKE A FARMER TO ME!

If you go to Stirling Castle and look at the statues which decorate the Palace building, take special note of the one which stands at the corner nearest the Great Hall. Among all the other figures dressed as important people, this one is a man wearing the ordinary clothes of a farmer. But above his head there is also a lion holding a crown—an important clue, for this is *actually* the statue of a king. So what is he doing dressed as a farmer?

The figure is King James the Fifth, who built the Palace part of the castle around the year AD 1540. When he became king, the royal money-chests were empty. He began to tax the rich nobles and eventually the royal money-chests became full, but you can imagine that he was not very popular with Scotland's lords! On the other hand, he seems to have been liked by the poorer folk. Perhaps they enjoyed seeing the rich lords brought down a peg or two by the king.

James seems to have enjoyed meeting the ordinary people of his kingdom. The problem was, if he wore the fancy robes of a king they would all bow and kneel and he would never really get to know them. So he decided to dress up as a 'gudeman' (pronounced like *good-man*) or farmer. When people asked him where he came from, he would say Ballengeich, which is the name of the little valley where the road runs nowadays between Stirling Castle and the cemetery on the Gowan Hill. And so, disguised as the 'Gudeman of Ballengeich', he would travel through the area meeting tinkers, outlaws, other farmers, folk from the town—and, they say, chatting up the girls!

Almost certainly people knew fine who he was. He may have dressed as a farmer, but he surely didn't have the worn hands of one. But he must have enjoyed the game, for the statue of the Gudeman of Ballengeich is still there on his palace for you to see today.

James V as 'The Gudeman of Ballengeich'

Chapter 11

Mary Queen of Scots at Stirling Castle

In the part of Stirling Castle called the Queen Anne garden, there is an unusual pointed stone in one wall. It has the letters M R carved on it, with a crown above the letters. The stone probably comes originally from an old window somewhere else in the castle, but what do the letters mean? Almost certainly they are the initials for 'Maria Regina', which is Latin for Queen Mary. This might refer to Mary of Guise, who was the French wife of King James the Fifth. More likely the letters stand for her daughter, the famous Mary, Queen of Scots.

Most people have heard of Mary, who was born at Linlithgow Palace in the year 1542. Her father, King James the Fifth, died just six days after her birth and so, at the age of less that one week, she became the new ruler of her country—Mary, Queen of Scots. What a life she had after that! And much of it was spent at Stirling Castle.

Even before Mary was a year old Henry the Eighth, the King of England, announced that he wanted the new baby queen to be promised in marriage to his five year old son Prince Edward. Some of the Scottish lords agreed to this, but others refused. They said this was just another way of England getting control of Scotland. Because there was danger of fighting between the various Scottish lords, the infant Mary was taken with her mother

DON'T YOU THINK SHE LOOKS QUITE **SAD**.

from Linlithgow Palace to the greater safety of Stirling Castle. There she spent the childhood years of her life.

On September 9th, in the year 1543, the nine month old queen was crowned in the Chapel Royal at Stirling Castle. That church is gone now, replaced by a newer one in 1594, but we are told from old records that the ceremony was not very costly. Some of the Scottish lords stayed away because they were protestant and Mary was a catholic—not a very good start to her reign.

Before long, things got even worse. Soon after Mary's coronation a row began with England. The Scottish lords refused to sign the marriage promise. In a fury, King Henry the Eighth sent his army to force Scotland to give in to his plans. In the years 1544 and 1545 the English attacked many places in the south of Scotland. Towns and villages, churches, abbeys and castles were all destroyed. Only Edinburgh Castle was not captured. This was called 'the rough wooing'—King Henry's attempt to 'persuade' young Mary to marry his son.

During these dangerous years the little queen lived in Stirling Castle. It must have been hard for her—not many playmates and little to do. So how did she pass the time? Some years ago workmen found a football stuck in the roof beams of an old part of the castle. You can see it on display in the Smith Museum. It's a very old ball—could it be one of Mary's toys? Certainly when she grew up Mary was very fond of sports, especially tennis, golf and archery.

If you visit the castle, have a special look at the walls in the Douglas Garden. There you will find a strange hole which, if you peer through, overlooks the King's Knot. Local legend says that this was made for the little queen, so that she could watch the exciting tournaments which were held in the field below the castle cliffs. At that time she was too small to see over the walls, but she must have been dying to look at the colourful scene below. Chapter 6 tells you about a famous tournament which was held there about a hundred years before Mary lived.

It is also said that the little queen sometimes visited the Holy Rude church, which was being enlarged at that time. No doubt she would have found the scene quite interesting—so many workmen doing different jobs—but she could not even talk to them. Remember that her mother was from France, so she grew up speaking French as her first language. In any case, she would have been surrounded by many bodyguards, probably pushing the workmen back rather than letting them talk to the queen.

Meanwhile, in 1547 the English army came on another rampage over the border. The Scottish army was totally defeated at the Battle of Pinkie, near Edinburgh. The provost of Stirling was one of many local men who were killed. Of course there was great worry in Stirling after that. The town walls, which you can still see if you follow the Back Walk, were hastily built in case the English tried to capture Stirling. Meanwhile, the five year old queen was secretly taken away from Stirling Castle and hidden at Inchmahome Priory, which is on a little island in the Lake of Menteith, near Aberfoyle. It was a scary time for people in Stirling.

How did it end? Well less than a year later the Scottish lords decided that Mary should marry the son of the French king. In August 1548, when she was only six years old, she left her mother and the bleak, draughty corridors of Stirling Castle, and sailed away to France.

What a time she had in France! She loved it— no danger, nice weather, a beautiful palace, friendly people. When she was fifteen she married Francis, the crown prince of France. When she was sixteen the king died, so her husband became the new king. That meant Mary was now the queen of Scotland *and* France! Then when she was seventeen her husband died, so she was no longer the queen of France. At the age of nineteen she sadly returned to Scotland.

As an adult Queen Mary sometimes returned to Stirling Castle. On one visit her bed curtains went on fire—she was saved by her maid-servant who dragged her to safety. Some people say that this is the 'Green Lady' ghost who is supposed to haunt the castle. In 1565 Mary fell in love with Lord Darnley while staying at Stirling Castle. They got married two months later and in 1566 they had a son called James. Like his mother, he was brought to live at Stirling Castle. Later he was christened in the Chapel Royal there—the same church where his mother was crowned as a baby in 1543.

So you can see, Stirling Castle has a lot of connections with Mary, Queen of Scots.

Chapter 12

The Medieval Town

Chapter Two told you that the town of Stirling was officially made into a royal burgh by King David the First, about the year AD 1124. At that time the town was very small—probably no more than the length of Broad Street! Let's look now at the town in the sixteenth century—around AD 1550, for example. Had it changed much by then?

As explained in Chapter 11, the town walls were built in 1547. They probably did not completely surround the town and the side facing the River Forth may only have been protected by a defensive ditch (although people's garden dykes would have made *some* kind of wall). The whole town was enclosed by the walls and ditch; nobody lived outside because it was too dangerous. You can still see part of the walls in Dumbarton Road.

The town had several gates (or *ports* as they were often known, from the French word 'la porte' meaning a door). They allowed people to pass in and out of the town through the walls. Stirling's main entrance was called the 'Barrasyett'. It stood where the traffic lights in Dumbarton Road and Port Street are now—indeed that's how Port Street got its name. If you look on the ground near the traffic lights you can see four metal blocks which are supposed to mark where the gateway entrance used to be. There were other gates into the town in Friar Street, Upper Bridge Street and where the Thistle shopping centre stands today. The gates were guarded, so everyone coming into the town could be checked if necessary.

Inside the town walls there were still not many streets in the town. Coming down hill from the castle, you would have passed along Castle Wynd before turning into either Broad Street or St John Street (which used to be called the Back Row). At the bottom of Broad Street, some houses were beginning to form the top end of St Mary's Wynd. There were probably also some houses at the top part of Spittal Street and Baker Street (which was called Baxter Wynd in those days, because 'Baxter' is the old Scottish word for 'baker'). Spittal Street may be named after Robert Spittal, a Stirling man who became famous around the year 1510 by becoming a tailor and clothes designer for the queen at Stirling Castle. What a small place Stirling was!

By 1550 the tolbooth stood in Broad Street next to the market cross (usually called by its Scottish name, the 'mercat cross'). Apart from the church, the tolbooth was the main building in the town. It was the court-house, town council meeting place and the prison. People were hanged or given other punishments just outside in Broad Street. The tolbooth also had a strong room where the town's money was kept in iron chests—banks had not been invented yet. The town guards also kept their weapons there. So you can see that it was an important place! It was probably first built about the year 1473 but by 1700 it was in such poor condition that it was demolished. The present building was constructed by 1705, so now it's nearly 300 years old.

About the year 1550 the present Church of the Holy Rood was just about finished. As you read in Chapter 7, the town, including its wooden church, was destroyed by the Earl of Douglas in 1452, so in 1456 a new stone church was begun. This building was completed about the year 1470, and today it is half of the Holy Rude church—the end nearest the castle. If you go inside, you can still see the old wooden roof beams which date from that time—the whole roof was built without using a single nail! About the year 1507 the other half of the church was built and this work ended about 1555. As you read in Chapter 11, Mary Queen of Scots sometimes came to watch the work going on when she was a child living in the castle.

In 1550 most buildings in the town were still made of wood and clay. As you can still see in Broad Street today, the houses had no front garden. However, each house had a long thin garden behind it—but not for growing flowers! People used these strips of land to grow food

or keep animals like cattle or pigs. Sometimes there was a shed for stabling a horse, or where craftsman like weavers or shoemakers could work—bakers were told to keep their ovens at the bottom of their gardens, well away from the wooden houses in case of fire.

The butchers did their work in the middle of St John Street, just down-hill from the end of the church. You could stand and watch the animals being killed with a long-handled axe. Then, as the dead beasts were cut open, the blood and guts ran down the street. On summer days when the weather was warmer, the smell from this mess was disgusting.

Something else also made the roads really mucky. No one had sinks or toilets in those days, so each evening you simply threw all your cooking, washing and toilet waste out the window into the street. In Edinburgh people shouted 'Gardy-loo' before they let fly, which gave anyone in the street time to scurry out of the way. We don't know if Stirling folk had a similar call or not. What we do know is that you did not want to live at the bottom of the hill! Just imagine what it must have been like when it rained—all the smelly butchers' waste, horse and cow droppings on the street, and household sewage was washed down the hill towards the bottom. No wonder rich people preferred to live at the *top* of the slope!

So when people talk about the 'good old days', just remember old Stirling. Would *you* have wanted to live in such a stinky place?

A view of Castle Wynd.

Chapter 13

John Cowane: a famous Stirling Merchant

Have you ever wondered who Cowane Street is named after? John Cowane was a rich merchant and is probably the most important person to have lived in old Stirling. He was born about the year AD 1570, almost certainly in the house in St Mary's Wynd which is still called Cowane's House today (though it was smaller in those days). By the time he died in 1633 he had become a very rich man, a member of Parliament, and someone who had met the king several times.

Like his father and grandfather, John Cowane was a merchant—someone who traded or sold things. Like most other Scottish merchants of that time, he did not specialise in selling any one particular kind of product (like cloth, or wine, for example). He sold anything he could—if you had

visited his wooden booth, or shop, at the bottom end of Broad Street you would probably have found all kinds of goods for sale, ranging from French wines and brandies or dried fruits from India or China, to musical instruments, expensive jewellery, guns and swords, sugar and spices, silks and velvets or fine carved furniture.

Many of these luxury goods came from abroad, and some merchants also owned the ships which brought these exotic cargoes to Scottish ports. One ship-load of wine or spices or silk could make a fortune for any merchant but, on the other hand, if his ship was sunk in a storm or captured by pirates, he could be ruined. As a result, merchants usually preferred to share the cost of a ship with a group of others, so if it sank no-one would lose too

much money. John Cowane was typical—at one point in his life he owned a sixth of one ship and one-eighth of another, and later he was part-owner of several more ships.

The harbour at Stirling was where Shore Road is now. Today you can only see a grassy area and the bollards where ships tied their mooring ropes. Only quite small ships could tie up there because the river was quite shallow—you can still see that for yourself if you look at the river when the tide is low. Big loops and bends on the river also made it very awkward for ships to navigate as far as Stirling—imagine how difficult it must have been if you needed the wind to fill your sails, but you kept changing direction because of the river's bends.

In spite of this, ships traded between Stirling and many different countries. Sawn wooden planks came from Norway, wine from France, bales of fine cloth from Belgium, grain from Poland, tobacco from London, iron goods like spears and bells from Holland, and so on. Most trade was with the town of Campvere (now called Veere) in Holland—in fact many Scottish merchants could speak Dutch! A large group of Scottish merchants lived in Campvere, and they organised cargoes of all kinds for sending across the North Sea to their home ports. John Cowane visited Campvere several times but he also traded a lot with Germany.

What kind of goods did a merchant like John Cowane sell to these foreign countries? The old records of Stirling tell us that it was mostly bales of rough cloth and piles of animal skins from cattle, sheep, goats and foxes—not very impressive!

If you had walked through old Stirling, you would easily have spotted the merchants of the town. They were much richer than most folk, so they dressed better with expensive materials in their clothes. Merchants also wore tall hats—all other men had to wear bonnets or berets, usually made of blue wool. In 1625 some people came on a visit to Stirling from Campvere. It was important to impress these foreign visitors and all the town's merchants were reminded to wear their best clothes—so you can imagine the reaction when two merchants were seen wearing bonnets! They were taken to court and fined for not being dressed properly.

John Cowane never married, so when he died in 1633 he left most of his money to the town. He wanted to build a place where merchants or their families could live if their business was ruined and they became very poor. It was called Cowane's Hospital (even though it wasn't for sick people) and you can still see it today. It stands next to the Church of the Holy Rood and it was built between 1637 and 1649. Nowadays the interior has been completely changed but it used to have seven small bedrooms and a dining room for the poor folk who lived there.

THE HARBOUR AS IT WAS NEARLY A HUNDRED YEARS AGO.

If you look above the entrance door you will see a statue of John Cowane, made in 1649. It is believed to look very like him. You can see that he is well-dressed, with expensive clothes (including a fancy lace collar) and the proper tall hat of a merchant—definitely one of the rich people of the town.

The statue is nicknamed 'Staneybreeks' and they say that, exactly at 12 o'clock each Hogmanay, he jumps down from his perch above the door and dances around. Do *you* believe that?

Chapter 14

Market Day
in Old Stirling

Market days were probably the most interesting part of life in old Stirling. As well as local Stirling folk going to market, many people also came into town from the surrounding countryside, so it was a busy, lively time of animal noises and the cries of people selling things. The market was held each Wednesday and Saturday, which allowed people to buy their weekly household needs like bread, meat or candles (though they could also purchase general supplies like rolls of cloth, shoes or pots and pans).

Although some merchants (like John Cowane in Chapter 13) had a lock-up wooden shop or booth in Broad Street, the craftsmen who made the town's everyday goods usually had no shop. They had to set up temporary stalls on market days. These stalls were mostly around the mercat cross in Broad Street, or close by in Jail Wynd or St John Street. At that time the main road through Stirling entered the town at Port Street, passed up King Street and Baker Street and then turned right down St Mary's Wynd on its way to Stirling Bridge. In other words, the location of the market was away from the busy streets, so people could set up stalls without too much traffic coming and going at the same time.

Market days were really interesting and colourful. By 10 o'clock the bakers would have their stalls set up around the market cross and the smells of delicious new-baked bread, pies and honey-cakes would fill the air. Nearby would be other stalls displaying things like candles, shoes, bonnets or ribbons. Some stalls were piled with vegetables, chickens, cheese, fish or perhaps exciting things like raisins or figs from far-away lands.

Sometimes farmers came in from local farms with food to sell—chickens, pigs, geese or perhaps eggs—but they had to pay a *customs* charge at the town gates to be allowed to sell anything at the market. As Chapter 12 tells you, the main *port* or gate into Stirling was called the Barrasyett. It stood where the Dumbarton Road traffic lights are now. People paid their 'customs' money at this port—that's why there's a pub on the corner of the Craigs called the Port Customs Bar!

All goods had to be checked before going on sale. In those days people used old-fashioned weights and measures like the *ell*, which was a length (just less than one metre) used when selling cloth. Every cloth-seller had a straight stick exactly one ell long, to measure out the rolls of cloth, but if you disagreed you could check the seller's ell stick against the official stick kept by the town council. All weights were checked on the *tron*, which was a public weighing beam supervised by the weighmaster. So if a farmer came into town claiming that his cheese weighed, for example, one pound (0.45 kg) this could be verified on the weigh-beam. The tron probably stood in Broad Street near the tolbooth, so everyone could see it in use.

The quality of things for sale was also checked regularly by officials at the market. You could be fined in court if your bread was stale, or the shoes you made were badly stitched, or your beer was too watery. For example, in 1647 a butcher called Andrew Thomson was fined £5 by the court, for selling bad meat. It was important that people had faith in the quality of things sold at Stirling.

The price of all goods for sale was also controlled by the town council. In 1564, for example, the price of a pair of good boots was fixed at 24 shillings (£1.20p) while double-soled women's shoes cost 2 shillings and six pence (12½p). In 1598 the council decided that the price of a medium-sized loaf would be 5p, a pound of tallow candles would cost two shillings (10p), and beer would be one shilling (5p) per Scots pint—but that was the same as three English pints! Just like nowadays, prices went up in those days too. For example, by 1629 the same candles would have cost three shillings and eight pence (18p), the same loaf cost 6p and that Scots pint of beer was up to 7p.

Do you think these prices sound very cheap? It all depends on how much you earned. In 1642, for example, Duncan Ewing was paid £60 a year to be the town's drummer. That means he had just over £1 a week to spend. So if a loaf of bread cost 6 pence and a pint of beer was 7 pence, that would have been quite expensive for Duncan. On the other hand David Will, the local schoolmaster, was paid about £120 a year so he could afford these prices.

Broad Street must have been an interesting place on market days. There would have been crowds of people drifting around looking at things for sale—pottery mugs, wooden plates, iron tools, clay tobacco pipes. Then there were also men drinking in the pubs, perhaps celebrating a good buy or making a hard bargain with some craftsman. Outside in the street there would be the noise of animals lowing, musicians playing, folk buying and selling, perhaps the town crier with his bell making a public announcement from the steps of the mercat cross.

Outside the tolbooth someone was perhaps suffering a public punishment ordered by the court—market day was always a good time for that, because there were so many people there to watch. And, of course, with so many people in town there would probably also be pickpockets and thieves among them. In those days folk carried their money in a small bag or purse which hung from their belt, so it was easy for a 'cut-purse' with a sharp knife.

And strutting proudly among the ordinary folk would be the merchants; people like John Cowane, better dressed and easily noticed because they wore hats, whereas other men just wore poorer blue woollen bonnets. All part of the scene on market day in Stirling.

THIS IS WHERE THE **MARKETS** WERE HELD IN OLD STIRLING.

Broad Street in 1600.

Chapter 15

Law and Order in Old Stirling

On 17th December 1546 the court in Stirling's tolbooth heard the trial of John Fisher, a thief. He confessed that during the night of 5th December he had stolen clothes from James McKeson who lived in Barn Road. He also admitted that he had broken into Alexander Alshinder's cellar and stolen a baked chicken and three cakes. He had also taken some malt and a basket from Bessie Smith's house, and had stolen 26 shillings (£1.30p which was quite a lot then) out of the purse of Thomas Millar from Menstrie.

Having been found guilty, this was Fisher's punishment. First he had his ear *nailed* to a wooden post in Broad Street—later this ear was *cut off* and left nailed to the post. Then he was *branded* on the cheek with a red-hot iron bar, *whipped* through the town, *thrown out* of the town gates and warned that if he ever came back again he would be *hanged*. Some punishment! You definitely did not want to break the law in old Stirling!

John Fisher's grizzly punishment was actually quite typical for that time. Most punishments were done in public, usually in Broad Street where there was room for a crowd to gather and watch. It was cheaper than putting someone in a prison cell in the tolbooth. And each punishment also taught everyone else a lesson—a reminder not to break the town's laws.

How do we *know* that John Fisher had his ear cut off? Well, it's written in the records of the court—old papers which you can still read today. And there are more examples of ear-cutting—in June 1545, for example, two thieves called William Brown and James Duncanson had their ears cut off before being thrown out of the town. On 2nd June 1699 the town hangman was paid £2 for cutting the ears off two men in Broad Street. And in 1723 the town paid three shillings to buy a knife for cutting Catherine McNab's ear off.

Just as today, there were different punishments depending on the crime. For example, if you said lies about someone, you had to come to the market cross in Broad Street and beg their forgiveness in public. Sometimes you also had to hold your tongue and call out 'False tongue you lied when you said . . .' In 1547 Marion Ray was found guilty of calling Agnes Henderson a thief. For this she was put into a big basket which was tied by a rope to a pole sticking out of the top of the tolbooth tower. She hung up there in full public view, no doubt suffering lots of cat-calls and jeers from people down on the street, until the magistrates thought she had learned her lesson.

Another way of teaching gossip women a lesson was to make them wear a 'branks'. This was an iron frame which fitted on your head like a hat, but with a flat piece of metal which jutted into your mouth. This stopped you from speaking—in other words, it was supposed to teach you not to spread untrue stories about people. In April 1654, for example, the town's officers led a woman wearing a branks through the town, so that everyone would see her. In October 1702 we know from the court records that Helen Cousland, wearing a branks, was also paraded through the streets by the officers. Unfortunately we don't know if she learned her lesson from this embarrassing experience.

If you go to the Smith Art Gallery and Museum in Dumbarton Road you will see the town's stocks on display. The stocks were kept in the tolbooth and carried out into Broad Street where people were made to sit with their feet through the holes. Again, the intention was to embarrass the victim by public humiliation. In July 1527 Robert Dougal was put into the stocks, but as late as 1723 old papers from the court tell us that the stocks were still being used.

Just as nowadays people got into trouble for fighting or causing a disturbance in the street. In 1545 a butcher called John Murray was arrested for stabbing Matthew Robson. He was told to leave the town or else spend a year and a day in the tolbooth prison. Then in 1560 Thomas Edwin attacked James Kirkwood with a golf club, and stabbed John Allan's wife with a knife. He was put imprisoned in the tolbooth. In 1599 James

Henderson, the son of a baker, cut the town officer with a knife, for which he was fined £10 (a lot of money in those days!). Then he had to go to the market cross and confess his crime in public.

Occasionally people were hanged. Although some were executed in Broad Street, the normal gallows probably stood roughly where the Black Boy fountain is today, near the Allan Park cinema. In those days, that would have been just outside the town gates, where travellers could see the bodies dangling from the gibbet. In 1525 Richard Brown was hanged there for stealing two horses from the Cornton. In the same year Robert Murray and James Muir were hanged for stealing clothes. Occasionally other people were executed there, usually for horse stealing, though in 1651 a man was hanged for murdering his child. At least five women were also hanged at Stirling. The old records of the court don't always give their names, but we do know that Elspeth Park was hanged in 1708 and Margaret Gillespie was executed in 1750.

Although these old punishments sound rather gruesome, the fact is that crime was fairly rare. Perhaps the fact that the punishments were so cruel was enough to stop most people from breaking the law!

Stocks and other ways of locking prisoners up.

Chapter 16

The Church of the Holy Rude

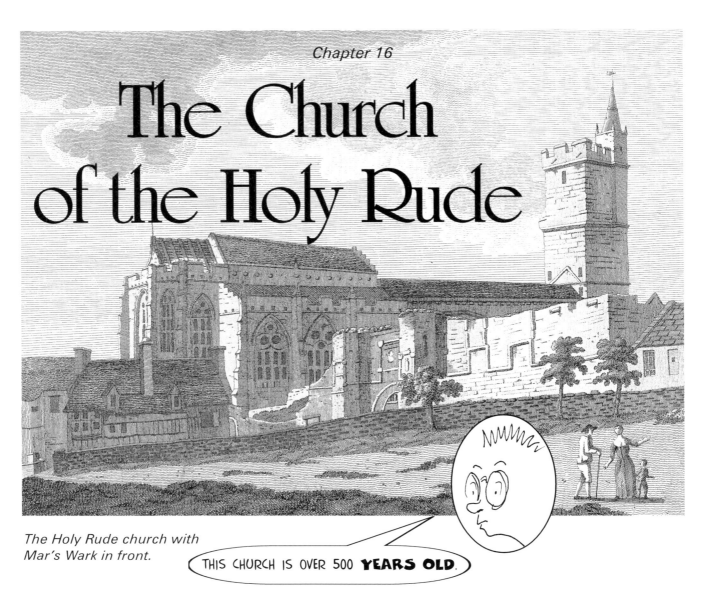

The Holy Rude church with Mar's Wark in front.

THIS CHURCH IS OVER 500 **YEARS OLD**.

Stirling may be quite a small town in Scotland, but it has one of the greatest medieval churches in the land. Chapter 12 tells you when it was built.

The Church was completed about the year 1555. At that time Scotland was still a Roman Catholic country, so the church would have been full of little chapels, statues and flickering candles. The priests would have worn colourful robes, especially on special religious feast days. There were no wooden benches or chairs, so the interior of the church would have looked much emptier than it does today.

In those days the door was at the end of church, so processions could enter at one end and move up the centre of the building to the altar at the other end. This door is blocked up now, but if you go outside and look carefully you can still see the bottom of two carved pillars which show you where the door was, and how wide it used to be.

In 1559 the Protestant form of Christianity began to be used in Scotland. This time is called the Reformation. In Stirling, people went to their church and cleared out all the old Roman Catholic decorations. You can still see the empty spaces on the walls outside where statues used to stand. Inside, only one chapel still survives nowadays.

After that the church was changed into a place where Protestants could worship. Instead of having an altar at the top end of the building, the ministers used a pulpit placed more in the centre, so that people could hear the sermons on all sides. Some of the more important folk had 'lofts' or balconies built inside the church. There was one for the craftsmen, another for the merchants, some for local landowners and one for the king. These are all gone now.

On 29th July 1567 King James the Sixth was crowned in the church. He was only a year old when his mother, Mary Queen of Scots, escaped to England and he became king. A plaque on the floor marks the place where the infant king was crowned—actually, he was far too small to have a crown placed on his head, but the Earl of Mar held it above him instead.

Chapter 17

The English Capture Stirling

You probably know that in 1649 King Charles the First had his head cut off in London. This came after a civil war between the Cavaliers (supporters of King Charles) and the Roundheads led by Oliver Cromwell. After the king's execution, Oliver Cromwell became the leader (he called himself the 'Protector') of England.

In Scotland the people wanted the dead king's son (also called Charles) to be the next king. He was crowned at Scone, near Perth, in 1650 and became King Charles the Second. In England, Cromwell was very angry about this. He ordered General Monck and the Roundhead army to attack Scotland. The king escaped to France, but the Scottish army was defeated at the Battle of Dunbar in 1651. Soon the English army was camped outside Stirling.

Faced with a strong army of about five thousand battle-hardened troops, the people realised that their town walls would not keep them out for long. Wisely, they decided to surrender without a fight, and on August 8th 1651 the English troops marched into the town and took it over. They continued to occupy Stirling for the next nine years.

However, just because the town had surrendered did not mean that the castle had to give in as well. The castle garrison barred the gates and waited for a siege.

Using covering musket fire from the tower of the Holy Rude church, the Roundhead soldiers began to dig platforms in the cemetery for their cannons. You can still see bullet marks all over the church tower, made by musket balls fired by defenders in the castle at this time. You can also see bullet marks where the English shots hit the castle walls.

The siege itself was short. Not only did General Monck's cannons smash down the entrance towers of the castle, but he also had mortars—short stumpy cannons which fired high into the sky. They could fire right over the walls to explode in the very centre of the castle—you can still see damage marks made by some of these bursting cannon balls on the walls of the Chapel Royal in the castle. Realising that they were out-gunned and not safe anywhere within the castle walls, the three hundred highland troops which made up the defence garrison surrendered and marched out after only three days.

The gates of Stirling Castle in 1781.

Chapter 18

Looking after the Poor in Old Stirling

How do poor people live in Stirling nowadays? Fortunately there are lots of ways they can receive help. If they have no job they may get unemployment money from the social security, or a rent allowance for their house. They don't pay for medical care. Children may receive free school meals or clothing vouchers. Nowadays, because of this help, there is usually no need for poor people to starve or to be homeless. In *old* Stirling, of course, it was not like that.

Nowadays you sometimes still see young homeless people begging in the streets or sleeping in doorways, but it was much worse long ago. So many dangers could make a person poor in those days. Plague might kill your parents—if no one else could look after you, begging was the only choice left. A soldier might have an arm shot off in battle, so he could not work. Because there was no social security at that time, all he could do was beg. A merchant could die of illness—there were no insurance policies in those days, so his wife would have nothing to live off. This once-rich woman would now be a beggar. You might be deaf, or blind, or crippled, or mentally disabled in some way. You got *no* help for these things—so you had to beg to live.

If you had walked through the streets of Stirling, say about three or four hundred years ago, you would have seen some people who were so poor that they had to beg. They just sat on the streets asking passers-by for money. It was a very sad sight. Of course people in Stirling were not heartless. Some tried to help them. The Catholic church used to give gave *alms* to people—food, clothing or money perhaps. So did rich people in the town— one example was Robert Spittal.

Robert Spittal (born about 1480, died 1550) was a craftsman tailor who became rich in the early sixteenth century as a dressmaker for Queen Margaret at Stirling Castle. He used his wealth to start a 'hospital' or charity home for poor people, especially craftsmen, in Stirling. It opened somewhere about the year 1530 and was built where Irvine Place is now. In those days that part of

Stirling was just outside the town in what they called 'the hills'. This 'hospital' looked after about twelve people, mostly men. They lived there and were also given clothes, food and cooking pots. In return, they had to wear blue or grey capes, which showed that they were from Spittal's home. They did not like doing this because it showed they were poor.

About 1660 this hospital moved to where the Highland Hotel is now in Spittal Street. If you go along the Back Walk, you can still see an old plaque on the wall of the hotel which says:

> Erected in honour of Robert Spettall, Taylor to King James the Fourth, Donor of the Hospital in the Burgh for Relief of Decayed Tradesmen

'Decayed tradesmen' was an old-fashioned way of saying craftsmen (such as bakers or tailors or weavers) who had become poor. Sometimes the trade guilds tried to help their own members, and the Guildry helped merchants' families who fell on hard times. But there was never much money to help anyone.

Chapter 13 tells you that another famous man in Stirling was John Cowane, a rich merchant. He lived from about 1570 to his death in 1633. When John Cowane died, he left enough money to start another 'hospital' like Robert Spittal's. It was built beside the Holy Rude Church and you can still see Cowane's Hospital today. As explained in Chapter 13, it was used to help the families of poor merchants—remember, it only needed some war, or a ship to sink, or plague to come to town, for a merchant's life to be ruined. Merchants may have been the rich folk of Stirling, but they could also become poor quite suddenly.

But what if you were just an ordinary person who became poor? What if you did not qualify to live in Spittal's Hospital or Cowane's Hospital? Who looked after you?

The church tried its best. Every Sunday the ordinary people who went to church services put a little money into the 'poor box'. This money was used to help the most needy people in town. During normal times, this was just about enough. But what happened if some great calamity happened, like fire or plague? What if lots of people were suddenly poor?

In 1699, for example, there was a terrible famine all over Scotland. The farm crops did not ripen. Thousands of people were starving and many came into Stirling hoping to get help. Soon there were so many 'stranger' beggars that the town council even had to make two hundred official metal badges for its own beggars. Most of the 'strangers' were thrown out of town, so that the council could concentrate on helping its own poor people.

How do we really *know* what happened? The proof is in the old books which were kept at that time. Let's look, for example, at the records of the Holy Rude church.

On Sunday 28th of May 1699, the church treasurer gave money from the poor box to over 150 people, 'being almost starving by reason of the present scarcity in the land'. He wrote all their names in his book, beginning with 'to Hugh McKenzie a stranger, 14 shillings and 3 pence' (about 72p). The list for that week includes many mothers and children, two blind women, an orphan, the town hangman and even seven prisoners in the tolbooth. The list ends by saying 'distributed at the Church door amongst a number of small ones, 2 pounds, 5 shillings and 3 pence' (about £2.27p). But remember, that was just one week. The church had to try and help people *every* week. Sometimes there was not enough. It was not easy being poor.

I THOUGHT A **HOSPITAL** WAS FOR **SICK** PEOPLE!

Cowane's Hospital.

Chapter 19

Plague in the Town

Plague was one of the worst things which could happen to any town long ago. It was an illness which spread quickly among people. If a plague happened, hundreds of people were likely to die, especially in towns where folk were more crowded together.

There were two kinds of plague. One was called the Bubonic Plague and was caused by fleas which lived in the hair of rats. If a flea bit you, you would get horrible, sore swellings and boils all over your body which could last for weeks. You had a 60% chance of dying, so you can imagine that people were terrified of catching it. Of course, in those days no-one had any idea that the plague was linked to rats—after all, there were rats everywhere, in every town.

They were so normal in people's lives. The other kind of plague was even worse. It was called Pneumonic Plague and it could kill you in less than one day, so it was *really* scary. It was passed from person to person in droplets, for example when people sneezed, or kissed, or used the same cup to drink from. If you caught it, it began as a pain in the lungs, but then it quickly spread through the rest of your body. Within hours you would have blood bursting from your ears and nose, even from your eyes.

In those days no-one knew what caused plagues—not even the best doctors. All they knew was that it was deadly and it could spread very quickly. If you caught it you had to stay indoors, well away from anyone else. This was for the wider good of the town. If someone in your house died of the plague, the body was collected and carted to a 'plague pit'—a big hole dug well away from town—

and there it was just dumped with all the others. Plague victims were not given a proper church burial and they did not even have a gravestone. How would *you* feel if your parents were just wrapped in a piece of cloth, laid in a big hole without even a coffin, and covered over? It happened to many young people in Stirling.

Plague came many times to Stirling. Most of Scotland was attacked by the terrible Black Death in 1349 and again in 1361. Although Stirling's records don't go back that far, the town was almost certainly affected, just like everywhere else. We know that the plague or 'pest' came again in 1546, 1548 and 1549. The town's old records say, for example, that in 1549 James Hall was put in prison because, when one of his servants got the plague, he did not destroy all of his clothes and possessions. He was supposed to do this as a safety measure for the rest of the town.

In 1606 another terrible plague struck the town. About 600 people died—that was probably more than one-third of the entire population of the town. Can you *imagine* such a disaster happening to Stirling? During this plague, all strangers were kicked out of town, and the town guards stopped anyone from coming in from plague-infected places. A special 'pest-house' was built for plague sufferers at Bridgehaugh (which was then well out of town). Of course, these things did no good at all.

In 1645 yet another plague hit the town. Four gravediggers (including two women) were paid to bury the bodies in a 'pest pit' roughly where the council offices at Viewforth are now. We should be very glad that plagues don't come to Stirling any more.

STIRLING PEOPLE WERE **TERRIFIED** OF PLAGUE: NO WONDER!

Chapter 20

The Old Graveyard

I KNOW HOW TO EXPLORE THE OLD GRAVEYARD NOW!

Have you ever been to the old graveyard which lies beside the Holy Rude church at the top of the town? It's a very interesting place, which tells us a lot about life in Stirling long ago. Some of the gravestones are hundreds of years old. If you look at these headstones nowadays, you will see many interesting carvings on them. You will usually see the year when the person died, and the initials of the people who lie buried there. In those days, wives were given the initials of their maiden name and not their married name!

On many of the older gravestones you will also see other markings. Many have a skull and crossed bones on them. If you think it's a pirate or someone who died of plague—wrong! The skull and bones are simply a sign to remind us that death comes to everyone sooner or later. Another sign of death is the hour-glass, which tells us that the sands of time have run out for the person who lies buried there. Many gravestones have an hour-glass carved on them. On the other hand, the stones also say that there is life after death, in heaven. They show this with signs for new life, like green leaves, flowers and angels.

Many gravestones also show the working tools of the person who lies there. For example, if you go up the main steps beside the door of the Holy Rude church, and walk about 7 metres straight forward, you will see the gravestone of Archibald Gilchrist and Isbal Paterson. If you look on the other side of this stone you will find a strange sign—it is the cutting blade or *coulter* of an old plough, which tells us that Gilchrist was a farmer. If you walk another 2 metres forward you will find William Maclean's gravestone. It has a brush, spade and shovel on it, crossed like a star—the tools of a *maltman* or brewer of beer. The brush was for stirring the beer.

If you keep looking around, you will find several stones with a shuttle carved on them—the sign of a cloth weaver. There are also stones with hammers on them, always with a fancy crown above the hammer. They show where a *hammerman* or metal worker has been buried. Keep looking and you may find a stone with a builder's tools on it, and another with a plant pruning knife—the sign of a gardener. Look for a stone now lying flat near the church tower. If you clear away the rabbit droppings you should see a pair of gloves—this man was a glove-maker.

The nearest stone to the church tower has an iron rail round it. It shows where John Cowane (see Chapter 13) lies buried. On the stone you will see a strange back-to-front figure four. This is the sign of a merchant, and you should be able to find several more like it. It's surprising how much you can learn from an old graveyard!

A merchant

A baker

A weaver

Chapter 21

The Battle of Sheriffmuir

In November 1715 a great battle was fought very near Stirling, up the slopes behind Dunblane on Sheriffmuir. You can still see a memorial stone there today, and if you look carefully in the fields nearby you can still see places where hundreds of dead men were buried. So what was it all about?

Back in 1688 King James the Seventh of Scotland, (but who was also King James the Second of England) was forced to give up his throne. The English threw him out for being too Catholic for their liking—remember that in 1649 they chopped King Charles the First's head off for the same thing. Like many Scottish monarchs before him, James went to France. There he lived in exile, hoping that one day he would get his kingdoms back. Meanwhile the English invited King William of Holland, who was a Protestant, to come and be the new king. Soon he was also accepted by most Scots as the new king of Scotland.

Some people, especially in England, were delighted to see the last of King James. But there were others, mostly in the Catholic parts of Scotland and Ireland, who said that it all completely illegal. Even if you did not like a king, they said, you could not throw him out because he had been given that position by God and you could not go against God's will. So he did have supporters in Scotland—people who did not want King William as their new king. They were called Jacobites (from *Jacobus*, which is the Latin word for James).

While the ex-king James lived in France, his son James grew up there. This younger James was the father of the famous Bonnie Prince Charlie. When King James died, still in France, the Jacobites in Scotland proclaimed his son 'King James the Eighth', (though he was never actually crowned king). Mostly these supporters were highlanders.

One of the strongest supporters of 'King James the Eighth' was the Earl of Mar. The Mar family was famous in Stirling—you can still see the ruins of Mar's Wark, the grand house built by a previous Earl of Mar, at the top of Broad Street.

By August 1715 the Earl of Mar was in the highlands organising the clans into a rebel army. Unfortunately for them, they took weeks to get ready, and by winter when they marched south towards Stirling, the British Army had rounded up enough men to fight them. The two sides met on a bitterly cold frosty morning on Sunday 13th November, on the bleak moorlands of Sheriffmuir.

Both sides were arranged in two lines. The 3500 red-coated army soldiers formed up in regiments with their backs to Stirling. They were commanded by the Duke of Argyll, an experienced soldier whose fine house, Argyll's Lodging, still

The Gathering Stone.

stands in Stirling nearly opposite Mar's Wark. The Jacobites, numbering about 8000 kilted highland clansmen and lowland peasants in their dull grey clothing, stood in battalions opposite them, with the MacDonald, Maclean and Gordon clans in the centre of the front line.

The battle started at about midday, when the left-hand end of the clans' line suddenly attacked the men opposite them. 2000 clansmen advanced and fired their muskets once. Then they threw their guns away, drew their broadswords, and charged with a terrifying assault into the red-coats. The army soldiers were only saved when Colonel Cathcart led a cavalry charge across the frozen marshland, which made the highlanders turn and flee. They were chased towards Greenloaning, where their escape was cut off by the River Allan and many were killed. Most of Clan MacRae fell beside the river. So in this part of the battle the British Army was successful.

However, while this was going on, the other end of the Jacobite line was also attacking the red-coats. They did much better. By getting round the side of the soldiers, they were able to surround them and most of the red-coats here were wiped out. In just seven minutes, an attack by the MacDonalds forced many of the army troops to flee for their lives, chased through Dunblane and Bridge of Allan by the highlanders. From the walls of Stirling Castle the garrison watched as their men were seen running in panic through the fields where Cornton is now, desperately trying to make it to the old bridge and safety on the other side. Up in the castle, they thought they had lost.

In fact, both sides were losing and winning at the same time. It was a draw. They say that each side had about 600 men killed—a terrible loss. That night, although they had not been defeated in the battle, the Jacobite army began to retreat back towards Perth. 'King James the Eighth' landed in Scotland soon after, but he quickly realised that the rebellion had no chance now and a few weeks later he sailed back to France. He never returned.

So now you know how the Battle of Sherrifmuir stopped the father of Bonnie Prince Charlie from becoming the king of Scotland.

THIS IS WHERE THE HIGHLAND SOLDIERS ARE SAID TO HAVE SHARPENED THEIR SWORDS BEFORE THE BATTLE.

Chapter 22

Bonnie Prince Charlie at Stirling

The siege of
Stirling Castle.

I'm sure you've heard of Bonnie Prince Charlie or, to give him his correct name, Prince Charles Edward Stuart. He's one of the most colourful and famous names of Scottish history and, of course, he's another who came to Stirling. But why?

In the last chapter you read how his father, 'King James the Eighth', failed to become the king of Scotland because of the Battle of Sheriffmuir. After that James went back to France to live in exile. There he married and had a son called Charles—the Bonnie Prince we have all heard about. When Prince Charles was 25 years old he decided to come secretly to Scotland and try again with another rebellion to make his father king.

To begin with all went well. Although he brought no army with him from France, most of the highland clans again decided to support him. With an army of Jacobite clansmen he set off south. There he captured Edinburgh, beat the British Army at the battle of Prestonpans and marched on into England. He might have made it to London but we will never know—his men got fed up and decided to turn back at Derby. And so they headed north again, towards their homes in the highland glens.

THE GUNS WERE IN THE WRONG PLACE, SO THE ATTACK **FAILED**.

It is important to remember that *not* everyone in Scotland supported Charlie. Most of the highland clans fought for him, but he found very little sympathy or support in the lowlands. People there were loyal to the British government. So as he retreated back through Scotland, few joined his army. Charles actually had to force the folk of Glasgow at gunpoint to give his men shoes and clothing for the march home.

From Glasgow he headed for Stirling, where he hoped to cross the River Forth. There were just two wee problems—the people of Stirling didn't support him either, and the castle's cannons could fire at anyone trying to cross the bridge. Then in December 1745, as the Jacobite army drew closer, the commander of the castle decided to blow up one arch of the bridge (the one nearest the Raploch). This greatly upset folk in the town, for when Charlie and his men finally went away again, what would they do without a bridge?

The first Jacobites appeared outside the walls of Stirling on 3rd January 1746. Next day many more arrived and eventually the town was surrounded. Soon thousands of rebels were gathered for a siege. From the walls people could see cannons being dragged into position to fire into the town.

On the 6th January Prince Charles sent a letter demanding that the town must surrender immediately. What was the council to do? The town had no cannons to fire back with. The town guard had been on duty for three days and nights. Even the highest count of defenders came to only 900—against about 9000 Jacobites now outside. It was also winter and people were hungry. Meanwhile the Jacobite cannons fired twenty-seven shots into the town, which damaged some houses. The position was obviously hopeless and, wisely, the council decided to give in. On 8th January the gates were opened and the Jacobites marched in.

Many people in the town were furious that the council had surrendered without a fight, but looking back now, it was surely the best thing to do. If the Jacobites had captured the town by force, they would probably have killed many people and helped themselves to anything they fancied. As it was, that did not happen. The town now came under strict military law. People were warned that anyone going near the castle, or disobeying any rule, would be executed. Meanwhile, Charles set up his headquarters in a pub in Bow Street and wondered how to capture the castle.

Just as General Monck had done in 1651, he decided to set up his cannons in the cemetery near the Holy Rude church. To attack from two sides, he also placed some cannons on the Gowan Hill side of the castle, but here the soil was not very deep and the gunners could not dig gun emplacements. By 29th January everything was ready, but when the Jacobite cannons started firing, the castle's guns replied and in a few minutes Charles' artillery was completely wrecked. In other words, the attempted siege of the castle was a total failure.

By this time the British Army was getting close, so Charles decided to pull out of Stirling and continue north into the highlands. Since they could not use Stirling Bridge (with its blown-up arch) the Jacobites had to withdraw towards Kippen where they could wade across the River Forth on foot. On the morning of 1st February 1746, just as the last rebels were leaving the town, there was a loud explosion at St Ninians. The Jacobites had been using the church there as a gunpowder store— was it an accident, or did they deliberately blow up the building before setting off? Whatever the reason, only the church tower remains today—a silent reminder of the time when Bonnie Prince Charlie came to Stirling.

Next day the British army marched into town. The Duke of Cumberland, in charge of the soldiers, was given a special welcome—most local people were glad to see the back of Charlie and his highland men.

Chapter 23

Stage Coach Travel

How do you get around these days? Mostly by car, or do you sometimes go by bus or train? Perhaps you have a bike. But I bet you don't *walk* much!

200 years ago walking was the normal way of getting around. If you were rich you might have owned a horse but, in the days before railways, most people just walked. As a result, very few people ever went anywhere far from home. Unless you were a sailor or soldier, the chances were that if you were born in Stirling, you would marry someone from Stirling, live and work there all your life, and eventually die in Stirling—without *ever* travelling as far as Edinburgh or Glasgow or Perth!

Partly this was because the roads were dreadful. With so many ruts and pot-holes on the muddy surface, anything with wheels would probably get stuck or break a wheel. So there were very few coaches or carriages—even farmers often dragged their goods to market on a sledge rather than bother with a wheeled cart!

Eventually things improved. About 200 years ago they began to build better roads with hard surfaces—no tar yet, but at least they had gravel. You had to pay a charge or *toll* to use these new roads, but the money was partly used to provide workmen who kept the road surface in good repair. These new routes were called *turnpike* roads. They included the one which goes through Bannockburn, and the main road which still passes through Bridge of Allan. In 1794 Dumbarton Road became a turnpike road to Loch Lomond. In 1812 the Drip Road was built through the open fields of the Raploch area—now people could travel by this road and the Drip Bridge across the River Forth [to Doune or Callander].

Once the roads were improved, stage coaches began. With a team of fast horses pulling you, you could now travel much more quickly and comfortably to places all over Scotland. In 1792, for example, a newspaper printed this advert:

> The Stirling Light Coach sets off from Robert Lawson's inn, Grassmarket, Edinburgh, to George Towers's, Stirling on Mondays, Wednesdays and Fridays at 8 o'clock in the morning; and from George Towers's to Robert Lawson's likewise every Monday, Wednesday and Friday at 8 o'clock in the morning. The proprietors of the Stirling Coach mean to run her at the rate of six miles an hour for speedy conveyance of passengers. Each seat 8s. 6d. (about 42 pence).

There was no bus station in those days. As the advert shows you, coaches usually began at hotels in Stirling, so that passengers could stay there overnight before or after their journey. One of these was Wingate's Inn, now the Golden Lion in King Street.

Stirling also became a popular centre for tourist trips by stage coach. You could take a tour to the highlands or to Callander and the Trossachs, for example. So stage coaches were good for Stirling—*and* people didn't have to walk so much after that either!

THE FORTH AND THE CLYDE.
STIRLING AND LOCHLOMOND.
—
THE EAST AND THE WEST COAST UNITED BY THE STIRLING AND DUMBARTON TURNPIKE, A NEW AND MOST BEAUTIFUL ROUTE.

JAMES GRANT, COACH-PROPRIETOR, Stirling, will, on and after TUESDAY the 13th of July, run a splendid NEW COACH, called
THE FORTH AND THE CLYDE,

STAGE-COACHES OPENED UP THE **WORLD** TO PEOPLE IN STIRLING!

Chapter 24

THE BATTLE WASN'T BANNOCKBURN'S ONLY CLAIM TO FAME!

Bannockburn's Woollen Mills

Did you know that 200 years ago, almost all the tartan cloth in the world was made in Bannockburn? The spinning and weaving factories, or *mills*, have almost all been knocked down now, but they used to be very important.

200 years ago Bannockburn was already famous as a village of cloth makers. We know this because, in the year 1792, the local church minister wrote: 'For a long time, all the tartan used by the army has been manufactured at this village'. When you think of all the highland soldiers who wore kilts in the Scottish regiments of the army, that's a *lot* of tartan!

The tartan business was started in Bannockburn by a local man called William Wilson around the year 1770. To begin with the cloth was spun and woven by people in their own houses, but eventually the first woollen mills were built. They were situated around Robert Spittal's old bridge which still crosses the Bannock Burn down in the valley. This stream turned the mills' water-wheels, which worked the machinery inside each building.

Although only one old mill building survives today, by 1862 there were ten factories in that small area, and they employed over 700 people.

Many of these woollen workers were little children. In 1832 a factory inspector noted that Wilson had 47 children, aged between 8½ and 15 years old, working in his mills—can you *imagine* working at the age of only 8? In 1861 a local population count listed 50 boys and 110 girls working in Wilson's factories. They made mostly kilts and tartan shawls, which were very fashionable then. Children worked the same hours as the adult workers—from 6 o'clock in the morning to 8 o'clock at night! They must have been exhausted.

In 1832 a little girl called Jane Reid was asked what the work was like. She said: 'I like being at the mill fine. I can't say I'm very tired. I get licked (smacked) by some whiles but not much—just a skelp or so on the lug to keep me at work. I earn 2*s* 9*d* (about 14 pence) a week'. What a lousy life she must have had, making Bannockburn's famous tartan cloth.

This mill in Stirling was used to spin wool into yarn a hundred years ago.

Chapter 25

Nail Making at St Ninians

In the last chapter you read about the children who worked in the cloth mills at Bannockburn. But if you think *that* was a rotten job, wait till you read here about the young nailmakers of St Ninians!

Nails were made from long strands of wire. It was a specialist business which had been going on at Whins of Milton, near St Ninians, for a long time. In the year 1792 the church minister at St Ninians wrote that 'four masters employ about 113 hands (workers) in making nails'. By 1842 there were 182 nailmakers at Whins of Milton. Fifty-one of them were boys aged less the thirteen.

These boys had a terrible life. At nearby Camelon, which is part of Falkirk, there was a bigger nail-making trade—in fact there is still a street there called Nailer Row. Most of the boys who worked at Camelon were orphans, sent to live and work with a nail-maker because it was cheaper than keeping them in an orphanage. Some were only six or seven years old when they started work.

The Camelon boys worked an average of fifteen hours each day except Sunday. Normally they had to make at least two hundred nails before breakfast, another four or five hundred by lunch, and at least three or four hundred by tea-time. Younger boys were not even paid for this—it was enough just to be given a bed, food and clothes by their master. Many boys' ankles became bent because they stood for so long each day. Most of them wore only rags, because their master gave them only one new set of clothes each year.

Although it was not quite so bad at St Ninians, compared to the nail-maker boys of Camelon, they still had a dreadful life. The St Ninians boys were not usually orphans—most worked for their father, and they also received some education, so maybe their lives were a little better. But they still had to make at least 800 nails every day. In fact, the minister for St Ninians wrote that they usually made between 1000 and 1200 nails each day. Can you *imagine* how hard that must have been?

What *proof* is there that things were really so bad? One way to find out is to read official government inspection reports—*they* ought to be correct! In 1842 an inspector visited some of the nail-making workshops at St Ninians. He wanted to know what it was like for the children who worked there. When he questioned 11-year old John

Duncan, this is what the boy said: 'I work from six o'clock in the morning to about seven or eight o'clock at night. I make about 800 nails every day, but I could make 1000 if my father forced me'.

During the 1850s nail-making machines were invented. After that, the use of children gradually declined. Eventually the hand-made nail trade at St Ninians disappeared. There is no sign of it any more, nor anything to remind us of the sad little boys who once toiled there.

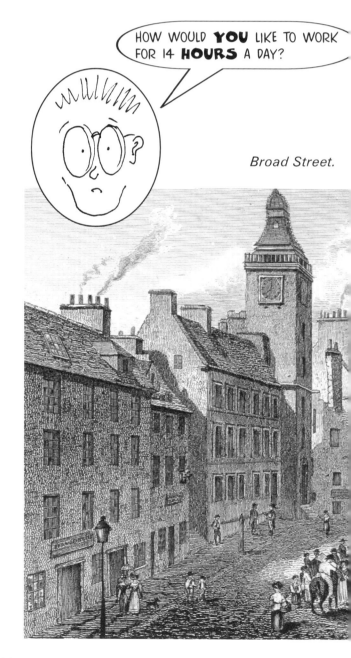

HOW WOULD **YOU** LIKE TO WORK FOR 14 **HOURS** A DAY?

Broad Street.

Chapter 26

The Last Public Execution in Stirling

On the night of 14th May 1843 Allan Mair, an old man of 84, murdered his wife in a cottage near the village of Muiravonside. He beat her so violently with a stick that she died later, covered with blood. So he was arrested and taken to a prison cell in Stirling's tolbooth. At his trial he was found guilty by the judge and sentenced to be hanged outside the tolbooth in Broad Street. It turned out to be the last public execution ever held in Stirling—why?

Local people were split over Mair's punishment. The judge said that even if Mair was old, he *had* murdered his wife. In those days that meant just one punishment—death. There were plenty of people who agreed. So did the local newspaper the *Stirling Journal*. On the other hand,

there were also folk who thought Mair should not be hanged. They said he was old and his mind was probably feeble when he killed his wife. Yes, he *should* be punished—but not hanged. Stirling's other local newspaper the *Stirling Observer* agreed. It said if Mair was put in prison, he would be a more lasting reminder to other people not to break the law.

The day of the execution came. On Wednesday 4th October 1843 Mair was brought out of the tolbooth at 8.27 am to the gibbet where he was to hang. He was so old and frightened that he had to be almost carried out by two law officers. With Mair came the hangman, wearing a huge black mask. By the time they reached the gallows Mair was so weak and terrified they had to bring him a chair to sit on, placed over the scaffold trapdoor.

Although it was raining, a large crowd had gathered to watch the hanging. To begin with the old man was allowed to speak to the people. From the scaffold platform he cursed and shouted that he was innocent, but no one believed him. Eventually the hangman placed a white hood over his head and fitted the noose round his neck. The local minister said a prayer. Then, with Mair still speaking inside the bag, the hangman pulled the lever which opened the trapdoor, and the body dropped. There was a cry of horror as he yanked one hand free and tried to grab onto the rope. For a moment he struggled to save himself, but eventually he went limp and still. Half an hour later the body was cut down and the murderer Mair was dead.

Most folk were upset at the sight of a grey-haired old man going to his death sitting on a chair, with his arms tied and a bag over his head. There were protests that this was too cruel for people to watch. So there were no more public hangings in Stirling.

Mair's body was buried inside the tolbooth. Nowadays they say he haunts the old prison part of the building—but only on Wednesdays, and mostly around the place where he lies. But I'm not telling where that is! The only way you'll know is to see the ghost for yourself.

HAVE **YOU** SEEN THE **GHOST** OF ALLAN MAIR?

Chapter 27

The Coming of the Railways

The 1st of March 1848 was a very important day for Stirling. On that day the town was linked for the first time by a railway to the outside world—or at least as far as the Edinburgh-Glasgow line at Castlecary. In May 1848 the other part of the line was also opened—now people could also travel as far as Perth by train. The journey to Perth took about 1½ hours by railway, which was much faster than any coach.

GRAND PLEASURE EXCURSION
TO
LOCH-LOMOND, BALLOCH, and DUMBARTON.

THE Committee of the Stirling Young Men's Abstinence Society have pleasure in announcing that they have made arrangements with the Forth and Clyde Railway Company for a PLEASURE TRIP to the above-named places

On SATURDAY the 9th AUGUST, 1856,

Leaving Stirling at .. .. .. 7.0 A.M.
Returning from Balloch at .. .. 6.30 P.M.
   The Steamers for Loch-Lomond leave Balloch on the arrival of the Train at 8.50 A.M., also at 12.50 P.M. Return Steamers leave the Top of the Loch at 2.15 and 3.30 P.M.
   Parties leaving by the 11 o'clock Steamer will have upwards of 2 hours at Balloch to view the beautiful grounds of Tilliechewan Castle, which, by the kindness of the Proprietor, Wm. Campbell, Esq., will be open to the excursionists.

TO DUMBARTON

By Trains leaving Balloch at 10.45 A.M., 1.30 3.30 P.M.
Returning from Dumbarton at .. 2.18 5.18 P.M.

FARES.

	3d Class.	1st Class.
Stirling to Balloch and Back, ...	2/	3/6
,, ,, Loch-Lomond and Back, ..	3/	4/6
Balloch to Dumbarton and Back, ..	0/6	0/9

   Tickets to be had from the following parties, and as only a limited number for Loch-Lomond will be issued, to prevent over-crowding, early application is necessary:—St Ninians: Mr T. Gardner, Post-office. Stirling: Mr Mann, Bootmaker, Baker Street; Mr Lochead, Refreshment Rooms, do.; Mr Hewit, Bookseller, King Street; Mr Mitchell, Clothier, King Street; Mr Ferguson, Bootmaker, Port Street; and from any Member of Committee.
   Should any Tickets remain unsold on Friday evening, they will be sold at the Station on the morning of the Excursion.

For three years the line had been under construction by hundreds of railway builders, or *navvies*, many from the highlands, England and Ireland. Local people dreaded these men, as the *Stirling Observer* described in January 1846:

> The men are thrown idle in wet weather, and on these occasions, and in the evenings, after their work is over, they lounge in the streets, or spend their time and their money in the public houses . . . very few of them attend any of the five churches in the town . . . many of them can neither read nor write.

Some of the navvies got drunk and then there was often trouble. Sometimes there were gang fights between highland and English navvies. Some drunk men tried to go shoplifting. Quite a few were arrested and appeared in court. John Mulligan, for example, was found guilty of stealing from a shop in Dunblane and was given a punishment of sixty days in prison.

They may have been rough, violent men, but their work was also very hard. Sometimes there were terrible accidents. For example, an Irishman called John McFadian was crushed by an earth-slip while working at Bridge of Allan—he was buried in the nearby Lecropt Church graveyard. At Greenloaning a 15-year-old local boy called Frederick Christie was run over by a railway truck—he died at Perth Infirmary before they could cut his legs off. Near Dunblane an Irish navvy was killed when dynamite exploded while he was examining the fuse. A man standing next to him had part of his skull blown off—but he lived.

The dead man was buried in Dunblane Cathedral graveyard. About 700 navvies came to the funeral. Afterward they all went into the local pubs and, according to the *Stirling Observer*:

> . . . during the evening the city was a complete scene of drunkenness and rioting, which continued through the course of the night and the whole of the next day.

You can imagine that the local people must have been very happy when the line was finally opened. Not only did it provide a fast and cheap way of travelling, but it meant that the navvies would be gone too.

In 1852 another line opened, this time from Stirling to Alloa and on to Dunfermline. The track still runs beside Causewayhead Road towards the Wallace Monument. This one was built by the Stirling and Dunfermline Railway Company, whereas the line to Perth was owned by the Scottish Central Railway Company. Since they were rival companies, they refused to share one bridge across the River Forth—which is why there are two, side-by-side.

In 1856 a line from Stirling to Balfron and Loch Lomond was opened. It cut through the Raploch area and out towards Gargunnock and Kippen. Although this line has been closed for many years, in some places you can still see where the rails used to lie.

Railways brought a huge difference to life in Stirling. You could now get to Glasgow in less than an hour (stagecoaches took over three hours). As a result, many Glasgow businessmen came to live in the lovely surroundings of Stirling rather than put up with the smoky environment of the big city. They built nice houses in the fashionable new King's Park area and commuted each day to work. That's the main reason why the King's Park area was built at all!

Tourists also flocked to the town. From Stirling you could take trips by stagecoach or railway to many beautiful parts of Scotland. New hotels, restaurants, toy shops, fishing tackle shops and lots of other facilities for visitors opened. Just think—if it hadn't been for railways, Stirling might never have become a popular tourist centre.

Another benefit was that local farmers could send their produce into town much more easily. Early every morning special trains collected containers of milk, left beside the track by farmers, and brought them in to Stirling so that people could have fresh milk from the town's dairies. Cattle could also be taken by rail to the cattle market. In those days it was in Wallace Street, where Tesco's stands today. Vegetables could reach Stirling shops still fresh and edible—good for farmers and local people alike.

The coal industry also benefitted. In those days towns like Alloa, Tullibody, Alva and Dollar were important coal mining places. The railway meant that they could send their coal easily and cheaply all over central Scotland.

But perhaps most important of all, local people had the chance to travel too. The railways were quite cheap and soon folk became used to visiting Glasgow or Edinburgh—places their forefathers hardly ever reached. They could take a train excursion to the seaside or the highlands. Railways opened up the world from Stirling.

LOOK AT THE HORSE-DRAWN CABS QUEUING UP LIKE TAXIS NOWADAYS.

Stirling Station c.1900.

Chapter 28

Bridge of Allan: a Victorian Spa

If you had visited Bridge of Allan any time before the year 1800, you would not have seen much. A small cluster of cottages around the Lecropt Church, a few houses near the old bridge across the River Allan, corn and paper mills beside the river where the Bridge Inn and Blairforkie Drive are now, a few farms such as Blackdub (where the Strathallan sheltered housing complex is now), and the tiny hamlet of Pathfoot near where the Meadowpark Hotel is today. There was nothing you could properly call a village. No shops or banks, no hotels—even Henderson Street, the main road through town, did not exist.

At that time, if you lived on the Dunblane side of the River Allan you were in Perthshire, so you would have gone to the Lecropt Church every Sunday. But if you lived on the Airthrey side of the river you had to go to the Logie Kirk, near the villages of Blairlogie and Menstrie, to worship on Sundays—there was not even a church where the village is now.

This quiet scene of white-washed houses was soon about to change, however. The one unusual feature of the village was its copper mine, whose tunnels burrowed into the wooded hills above the village where the Mine Woods still stand today. Long ago this mine provided copper for making Scottish coins, but by 1807 it was out of use. All that remained was a trickle of water which drained out of the tunnels. Local people said this water was good for their health and drank it from a wooden trough on Sunday mornings.

In 1820 the local landowner, Sir Robert Abercromby of Airthrey, decided to clear out the old tunnels and channel the spring water to a shaft approximately where Kipling's restaurant is now. There the water was specially pumped to the surface—but why? Abercromby had heard that a new fashion was spreading through Britain and Europe—people believed that drinking mineral water was good for you. So when the Professor of Chemistry at Glasgow University tested the water from Bridge of Allan and found that it was full of beneficial chemicals and minerals, Abercromby decided to sell it to visitors. And so began a new chapter in the history of Bridge of Allan—it's time as a famous spa, a place where people could come to drink mineral spring water as a cure for their illnesses.

Soon hundreds of visitors began to come to Bridge of Allan each year, anxious to buy the bottled water or bathe and shower in it. They needed somewhere to stay, so the first boarding houses and hotels began to appear. In 1842 the Royal Hotel was built. Then in 1848 the Stirling to Perth railway was opened and now people could reach Bridge of Allan by train. Carriages from the various local hotels used to meet railway travellers when they got off at Bridge of Allan's station. For a time Bridge of Allan was perhaps the most important health spa in Scotland. Among the famous people who came to the 'take the waters' were the famous Scottish writer Robert Louis Stevenson and the English author Charles Dickens.

Although the popularity of Bridge of Allan grew quickly, the village managed to keep its charm as a picturesque country place with quaint white cottages and beautiful scenery all around. By 1855 the population was only 1600 people—but that year about 30,000 people came to visit! A local street directory for 1866 listed five hotels and no fewer than 126 lodging houses! Many of the older buildings in the town, both 'up the hill' and down in the Keir Street area, were built originally as guesthouses for summer visitors.

These people also needed

things to do each day, just like any modern tourist resort. So bowling clubs, tennis courts, the golf club, a music hall, and several denominations of churches were provided. Visitors could also fish in the river, take walks through the pleasant local countryside, or perhaps visit the Wallace Monument which opened in 1869. Some took stagecoach trips to more distant sites of interest—Stirling Castle, along the Ochil Hills, or to popular highland places like Loch Lomond, the Trossachs or Blair Atholl.

The craze for taking mineral waters continued to grow. The Allanwater Hotel (now converted into private flats) was built in 1864 with a purpose-built suite of baths claimed to be the best in Scotland. Hundreds of people came to use this new facility. A weekly newspaper called the *Bridge of Allan Gazette* listed these visitors so that people would know 'who was in town'—these old papers make excellent evidence nowadays for historians to use.

In 1874 the first horse-drawn tram line in Scotland was opened. It started in Bridge of Allan at the foot of Mine Road, where the Clydesdale Bank is now. From there it went along Henderson Street to Causewayhead, along Causewayhead Road to the bridge, then up Wallace Street, and through Stirling by Barnton Street to the bottom of King Street. Later it was extended to St Ninians. So now people in Bridge of Allan could take a tram into Stirling if they wanted. The train was much quicker, taking only six or seven minutes compared to the tram which took about half an hour, but in summer it made a pleasant trip.

Eventually the fashion for taking spa water died out. People stopped visiting in such great numbers and Bridge of Allan declined to a sleepy village again. An attempt was made to revive the spa during the 1930s but that did not last long. The town only woke up again when Stirling University opened just along the road in 1967 and the place filled with new visitors—students.

THOUSANDS OF PEOPLE VISITED THE **SPA** EACH YEAR AND USED HOTELS LIKE THIS ONE.

The Allanwater Hotel.

Chapter 29

Shopping in Victorian Stirling

WOT! NO SHOPPING TROLLEYS?

A Victorian grocer's shop in Stirling.

Nowadays people shop at supermarkets, where you can buy most things under one roof. Meat, bread, vegetables, milk—even clothes and toys. But can you imagine having to go to a different shop for each of these things? That's what shopping was like in Victorian times.

In those days there were no shopping centres. Most shops in Stirling were in King Street or along Murray Place and Barnton Street. In 1881 the Arcade opened—that was a *kind* of shopping centre, I suppose, but even here the shops were all different kinds.

Sometimes street directories were printed—like phone directories nowadays, they helped people to find places in the town. The *Stirling Directory* for 1869 tells us that among the many shops in King Street there was a baker, a chemist, a saddle shop, a draper (which sold rolls of cloth) an ironmonger's (where you bought iron things like tools, nails, hooks etc), a bookshop, a jeweller, several dress shops, a china merchant (where you could buy nice plates, ornaments, tea sets etc), a knife and gun shop, a tobacconist, several grocers, a hat shop—and that doesn't even include the banks, photographer's, optician's or the hairdresser! Even in Friar Street, which was much less important, there was a fishmonger, a dairy, a toy shop, a hat shop, a shoe shop, two grocers and a butcher's shop.

The adverts for Victorian shops also tell us a lot. For example, Meiklejohn's in Baker Street boasted that it sold 'a large selection of bonnets, hats, dress caps, dress stuffs, flowers, feathers, ribbons, velvets, laces etc, all in the New styles'.

Alex Baird and Sons, umbrella and sun shade makers in Murray Place, sold 'the largest stock of fancy leather goods, toys, baskets, including all sorts of useful and ornamental articles to be found in Stirling.'

Prices were also *very* different from today! In 1885 a loaf cost 3 pence, a jar of marmalade was 1½ pence, a tin of peas was 2 pence, coffee cost 5 pence for 400 grams, malt whisky was 17 pence a bottle and beer cost 1 pence a pint. A man's suit cost £2, shirts varied from 5 pence to 15 pence, children's boots from 25 pence to 65 pence a pair, a brass bed cost £8 and a sofa was just £2. Although these prices sound very cheap, you must remember that a working man only earned about £1-£1.50 a week, and women usually made less. According to adverts in the *Stirling Observer*, shop girls made about 25 pence a week, while a servant girl in one of the big houses of the Kings Park area was paid about 40-50 pence a week. Prices are actually much cheaper now, compared to Victorian times, if you also look at how much people earn nowadays.

One interesting change in Victorian times was that shops sold things from all over the British Empire—tea from India, butter from New Zealand, silk from Hong Kong, spices from Africa, wool from Australia, bananas from the Caribbean islands, and so on. There was a much bigger selection of things than ever before. Only a hundred years earlier, Stirling folk still bought most everyday needs at the market in Broad Street, and most of what they bought was made by local craftsmen. Victorian Stirling's shops were *much* more interesting.

Chapter 30

Schools in Victorian Stirling

Did you know? Up to 1872 you didn't *have* to go to school at all! Most parents in Stirling did send their children to school for a few years, at least to learn to read and write, but it wasn't compulsory. In 1872 a new law forced children to attend school—but even then, it was only up to the age of 12. Can you imagine that?

There were several schools in Stirling for younger children. The most important was the Burgh School in Spittal Street, now Allan's Primary School, but there was also a small school in Cowane Street, a charity or 'Ragged' school in Spittal Street for poor children, an infant school in Murray Place and a school in Cambuskenneth. Some local churches also ran small schools—the Episcopal school in St Mary's Wynd and the Catholic school in Irvine Place. So it seems that parents in Stirling thought education was important for their children.

Most important of all was the High School. In 1854 it moved to a new building in Spittal Street—now the Highland Hotel. Although education became compulsory in 1872, you still had to pay for classes in those days. The fee was 37 pence per term—it doesn't seem a lot today, but it was expensive then. Only the children of well-off people like doctors or lawyers could afford the High School.

Most just left school as soon as they were twelve. Girls usually became either a house servant or a shop assistant when they left school, though some worked in the local woollen mills such as Hayford's Mill at Cambusbarron. If you were a boy there was a wider choice—in factories, as shopkeepers, on the railways or in various local crafts, for example.

In those days the High School taught only four subjects—English (but that included history and geography), Commercial (including arithmetic and book-keeping), Modern Languages (French, German or Italian) and Classics (Latin, ancient Greek, philosophy and astronomy—the observatory, still used today, was built in 1889). Later the choice widened to include drawing, music and the janitor taught gymnastics (better known nowadays as PE).

Very few girls went to the High School, although rich parents often sent their daughters to one of the local private 'schools for young ladies'. According to the 1869 street directory there were seven of these in Stirling. They taught 'ladylike' subjects like good books, foreign languages, religion, piano, good manners, and how to dance elegantly—the things a young lady had to know if she wished to catch a suitable husband. What a difference now!

Art class in Stirling High School a hundred years ago.

Chapter 31

Sickness and Health in Victorian Stirling

If you could travel back in time to the 'top of the town' part of Stirling about 150 years ago, you would surely notice at least two things. First, the streets were really mucky. Second, the houses in that part of town were really crowded. Because of these two things, if you were a poor person living in one of these crowded streets, the chances are that you would catch an illness and die before you were 50 years old. Some of your children would probably die before they were even five years old.

This chapter is all about people being ill. When was the last time *you* went to the doctor, or the hospital? We take it for granted nowadays. If you're ill—no problem! You just go along to the doctor and get some medicines. If you're *really* ill—still no problem! You get sent to the hospital and they look after you there. And it usually doesn't cost you anything either—it's mostly free! Everyone is entitled to medical care, no matter who they are.

But if you had lived 150 years ago in St Mary's Wynd, or Broad Street, or Spittal Street, or Castlehill, or one of the other crowded, smelly streets of Victorian Stirling, your life would have been *very* different. For a start, you would have lived in a house with no running water—if you wanted to wash, you had to join a queue to fetch water from a pump out in the street. Not surprisingly many folk didn't bother to wash much—and not surprisingly they got ill.

You would also have lived in a house with no toilet—just a pot which was kept under the bed, which everyone used. Guess what happened when it was full? Yes—*you* would have been sent to empty it onto the dungheap out in the street. Can you imagine if *every* family did that, *every* day? Yuck!

Let's look more closely at your house. Almost certainly your whole family would have lived in just two rooms, maybe even only one. You probably slept with several brothers and sisters in just one bed, probably in the kitchen. Your parents probably slept with the youngest children in the other room. That's called *overcrowding*. And that's how illnesses spread. Have you ever caught measles or chickenpox from someone else? Well just imagine how easy that would have been if you shared the same bed with several others!

Before we go any further, how do we *know* that the houses of Stirling's poor people were overcrowded? The evidence lies in the Census books of old Stirling. Every ten years, starting in 1801, the government made a check, called a *census*, of how many people lived in Britain. In towns all over the country, officials went round from house to house to make the check. They asked the names of everyone who lived in each house, and also how many rooms the house had. You can still see the books which they filled in as they went along.

Let's look at a real example. From the census of 1881 we know that the Hardie family lived at number 8 Broad Street. The parents were called Thomas and Sophia, and they had six children—Maggie aged 9, Elizabeth aged 8, Robert (7), Jessie (4), John (3) and Thomas aged 1. All of these people lived in just one room. And that does *not* even mean one room plus a kitchen and a bathroom. Everyone in the Hardie family had to wash, sleep, dress, cook, eat and do the toilet—all in just that one room. Can you imagine having absolutely no privacy?

What sort of illnesses did poor people catch in those days? Well, mostly they were

caused by germs—in the water, in food, on people's unwashed hands, in the smoky air, on the dungheaps outside in the street, on the feet of rats and mice and flies. Germs were everywhere. So people caught typhus, dysentery, tuberculosis and other killer infections.

The scariest illness of all was cholera. It was caused by germs in the drinking water which people got from the street pumps. Cholera could kill you in just a day or two.

Children often died from fevers, such as diphtheria, whooping cough and scarlet fever. Often they died just because they were poor. In those days it cost money to visit the doctor, and even more if he came to your house. Poor people could not afford any medical care, so they died.

Eventually things were done to improve people's health. During Victorian times the town council began to have the streets cleaned more often. The town's first water reservoir was built in 1848 and water became much safer to drink. The town council also tried to stop the overcrowding in some streets—they nailed a sign on each door stating how many people were allowed to live there, but many folk paid no attention and overcrowding continued.

In 1874 the town's first infirmary opened (although it cost money to go there for treatment). The original building still stands in Spittal Street, although nowadays it is the office of the Forth Valley Health Board. If you look carefully at the front you can still see where the letters 'Royal Infirmary' used to be fastened to the wall. The present Royal Infirmary was opened in 1924.

We've come a long way since the unhealthy, mucky days of Victorian times!

IMAGINE ONLY HAVING **ONE ROOM** TO LIVE IN!

Chapter 32

Stirling's Flying Pioneers

Did you know that some of the very first aeroplane flights ever seen in Scotland happened at Stirling? For this we must thank the Barnwell brothers, mostly forgotten now in Scotland except for Barnwell Road in Causewayhead.

Harold, Frank and Archibald Barnwell came from Balfron, but in 1907 they started the Grampian Engineering and Motor Company at Causewayhead (which is still there today). Although this was mostly for repairing motor cars and building engines, the Barnwells were also very interested in flying. They had already built gliders, and models of aeroplanes fitted with motor-bike engines. You must remember that the world's very first successful powered flight was made only in 1903, when the famous Wright brothers flew their aircraft about 40 metres at Kitty Hawk, North Carolina, in the USA. So these were still the very early years of flying experiments.

As well as founding the Grampian Company, the Barnwells also built an aircraft hangar where number 36 Easter Cornton Road is today. Here they built their first full-sized aeroplane in 1908, but the engine was not powerful enough for it to take off, so it failed. On Wednesday 28th July 1909, however, their next design made its first flight—a distance of about 80 metres, at an altitude of about four metres, from the field opposite the Birds and Bees restaurant. It ended up crashing nose-first into the ground, but pilot Harold was delighted, in spite of suffering a few cuts and bruises. After repairs, this plane managed another short flight in September, but the Barnwells decided that they needed a better design.

On Saturday 15th January 1910 another new plane was wheeled out of the big shed into the same field. With Frank piloting, it managed a flight of about 600 metres, circling over the Easter Cornton area. It was so promising that, on 30th January 1911, the plane was used again. This time, according to the *Stirling Journal*, it soared easily into the air and, with Harold at the controls, set off on a flight over Bridge of Allan at a height of about 60 metres. Unfortunately Harold turned too sharply and crashed into the Haws Park, but by then he had already travelled well over a mile—the first Scottish plane ever to fly that far.

The plane went on to fly several more times in the Blairdrummond area. The Barnwells went on to become famous aircraft designers during the First and Second World Wars.

THIS MAY BE FUZZY BUT THE PHOTOGRAPHER HAD **NEVER** SEEN ANYONE **FLY** BEFORE!

The first all Scottish plane to fly half a mile.

Chapter 33

The Suffragettes in Stirling

Nowadays, when you're sixteen you're allowed to get married. And when you're eighteen you can vote in elections for the Scottish parliament or the government in London. But it wasn't always like that. A hundred years ago, if you were a low-paid or unemployed man, you were not allowed to vote. And even worse—if you were a *female*, it didn't matter if you were rich or poor, clever or not, you were *certainly* not allowed to vote! Surely that was very unfair—after all, women are just as capable as men, *and* they form half the population.

Even in those days, some women thought it was wrong they were not allowed to vote. Led by Mrs Emmeline Pankhurst they formed an organisation called the Suffragettes. They wanted the government to change the law and give women the right to vote in elections—quite a task, considering the government was all *men*!

The Suffragettes were not the first women to demand the vote in Britain. The difference was, unlike the lady-like protesters of the past, they were prepared to play rough—they interrupted meetings, chained themselves to the railings of important buildings, vandalised golf courses, smashed shop windows, set houses on fire, blew up buildings and attacked politicians. Many were arrested and went to prison, but even there they continued to make news by going on hunger strike. Even if you didn't approve of their methods, you had to admit they were very good at getting publicity for their demands.

In those days the British Prime Minister was Mr Henry Campbell-Bannerman—the Member of Parliament for Stirling. So you can imagine that Stirling was one of the places where the Suffragettes were very active. They held huge meetings in various halls around the town—in May 1908, for example, the Albert Hall was filled with 2,000 people, *and* there were another 1,000 outside, unable to get in! Mrs Pankhurst herself came to Stirling several times to make speeches.

In August 1912 two Suffragettes from Edinburgh broke into the Wallace Monument and smashed the glass case in which William Wallace's famous sword was displayed. They did not steal the sword, but left a note saying that Wallace had fought for liberty and now women should fight for *their* liberty. Then in November 1913 Prime Minister Herbert Asquith was being driven in his car from Larbert to Stirling when he was stopped by Suffragettes just outside Bannockburn. They tried to throw pepper in his face but police stopped them before they did much harm.

Of course, there were many people in Stirling who did not support the Suffragettes. Even many women felt it was wrong to use violence or bombs to win their arguments. They held meetings too—Stirling must have been a lively place, thanks to the Suffragettes!

Women eventually got the vote in 1918—not really because of the Suffragettes, more because all women did a great job helping Britain to win the First World War. But at least the Suffragettes had everyone *talking* about votes for women first!

I KNOW WHY STIRLING WOMEN **ATTACKED** THE PRIME MINISTER!

Chapter 34

Stirling during the First World War

The First World War began in August 1914. For the next four years Britain, France, Russia and other countries struggled against Germany, Austria-Hungary, Bulgaria and Turkey. About 10 million soldiers, and another 10 million civilian people, died in that terrible war.

Although most of the fighting happened in Europe, Stirling was nevertheless caught up in the horrors of the war. If you look at the war memorial near the Albert Hall you will find the names of 692 Stirling men who were killed. There are 94 more on the Bannockburn memorial, 81 at Bridge of Allan, 37 at Cambusbarron and yet another 45 on the war memorial at Causewayhead. A lot of local men died. Many left wives and children.

In spite of that, there was an amazing rush by local men to join the army. Many joined the Argyll and Sutherland Highlanders regiment stationed at Stirling Castle—in fact, the castle held the record as the recruiting office where the most men enlisted for the war in one day in the whole of Britain. Not bad for a small town!

Many local buildings were used by the army during the war. For example, the Smith Museum became a cavalry store and St Ninians school became an army medical depot. An army training camp of wooden huts was built at Cornton (there were no houses there then), and military depots were built at Back o' Hill and Forthside. Two squadrons of fighter aircraft were even formed at Stirling. They flew from the flat fields around Falleninch Farm, near the fire station. The pilots trained to navigate by using the Wallace Monument and Stirling Castle as markers.

Apart from being unable to use some local buildings, people faced other restrictions in their normal lives. Every night they had to black out their windows in case German bombers came—though none ever did. But with shops, offices, churches, pubs and ordinary houses all blacked out, folk didn't go out much when it was dark. People's social life, such as going to the cinema or to dances, declined. Fewer trains ran, roads were not repaired, cars had no petrol, newspapers became smaller in size, and towards the end of the war there were also serious food shortages. Yes, the war affected ordinary people in Stirling quite a lot.

People were also very patriotic. Sometimes they hung British flags from their windows. In Riverside they changed the name of Coburg Street to Argyll Avenue because Coburg was a town in Germany. A popular teacher at the High School was forced to retire because he was German.

Women worked hard to help in the war. In Cambusbarron they made army uniforms at the Hayford Mills. In Stirling they collected money by holding fetes and selling snowdrops. They also made parcels of chocolates, books, cigarettes, woollen gloves and scarves to send to the soldiers in France. Some women delivered the mail or became conductresses on local trams, replacing men who had gone away to fight in the war. They did a great job.

On November 11th 1918 the war ended at last. Stirling people celebrated by ringing church bells, hanging flags from their windows, lighting up their windows, dancing and cheering in the streets. Later many went to church to give thanks that the terrible war was over.

Some of the first tanks toured Scotland to raise money and troops for the war effort. This tank named Julian *visited Stirling in 1918.*

Chapter 35

The first Council Houses in Stirling

It's strange but true. There are people who can still remember when some houses in Broad Street or St Mary's Wynd had *earth* floors and no electricity, toilet or running water. Can you *imagine* living in a house like that? Not in some primitive faraway country but right in the middle of Stirling!

After the First World War the houses in the old part of Stirling were in a terrible state. As Chapter 31 tells you, one big problem was overcrowding. This was made even worse by miners' families moving in when the Polmaise pits opened in 1904—the mining village of Fallin had not been built yet. As a result, in 1908 the average number of people per acre in Stirling was 14, but in Broad Street it was 290! Another serious problem was the quality of the houses. A local doctor said that at least one quarter of the houses in the Broad Street area were slums, unfit for human beings to live in—but people *did* live there. Something had to be done about it.

The answer was Council Houses. After the First World War the government offered money to help town councils build better houses. In 1919 Stirling's first council houses began to be built in the Shiphaugh area of Riverside. Compared to the dreadful houses of Broad Street, they were brilliant. 140 houses were built to start with—each with a living room, bedrooms, a separate kitchen, bathroom, electricity and even the luxury of hot water. People from the top of the town area moved in during 1920—to them their new homes were like palaces!

In the next few years lots more council houses were built, first at St Ninians and then along the Drip Road—the beginnings of the Raploch. Eventually over 2,000 new houses were built by the council. It was a tremendous achievement. Many people were able to move from their old slums into much better houses. The result was less overcrowding and less disease.

At the same time, the old houses in Broad Street, St Mary's Wynd, Castlehill and the other ancient streets of Stirling were demolished. Some people were very sorry, even angry, to see Stirling's historic buildings being knocked down. But they were *very* run-down and insanitary and they really *had* to go. Today the buildings which you see at the top of the town are mostly modern copies of old houses—but at least they are fit to live in.

Shiphaugh Place being built.

THESE **NEW HOUSES** IN RIVERSIDE WERE MUCH BETTER THAN HOMES IN THE OLD PARTS OF STIRLING.

Chapter 36

Stirling in the Second World War

On Sunday the 3rd of September 1939, the Second World War began. It was just twenty years since the First World War but once again life changed completely for the people of Stirling.

Some changes happened immediately. Even before the war actually began, local people were issued with gas masks in case the enemy dropped poison gas bombs (which never happened). On the very first day of the war a big British passenger ship called the *Athenia* was torpedoed on its way to Canada—some Stirling people died in that attack. Just as in the First World War, blackout regulations began again and Stirling became a dark town at night. Air raid sirens were tested. Church bells were stopped—from then on they were only to be rung as a warning if the Germans came.

Two days before the start of war, train-loads of *evacuee* children began to arrive from Glasgow. The government was afraid that big cities would be bombed by the Germans. They sent thousands of children to places which they thought would be safer. Hundreds came to Stirling and Bridge of Allan.

When they arrived at Stirling station they were first marched down Wallace Street to Orchard House in Union Street. There they were cleaned up with carbolic soap and water by local nurses and given a medical check. Doctors were afraid that they would carry diseases from their homes in the slums of Glasgow. Then they were shown to local people who picked the ones they liked the look of—can you imagine how *awful* you would feel if nobody picked you? Or if your family was split up? Then off they went with their new families to live in some strange house far from home. Many were frightened. Some were worried about their parents back in Glasgow. Poor folk didn't have phones in those days and it wasn't easy to keep in touch with home.

Since it was September, the children were soon sent to local schools for the new term. The classrooms were very crowded but teachers from their schools in Glasgow came to help the local teachers. If you talk to older people who remember the evacuee kids in Stirling, the most likely thing they will tell you is how rough they were—to begin with there was certainly a lot of trouble, including lots of playground fights. But eventually it settled down.

After a few months many of the evacuee children were taken home again. There had been no air raids on Glasgow and their parents thought it would be okay. How wrong they were! In 1940 and 1941 Glasgow suffered many heavy bombing attacks. At night you could see the orange glow of burning Glasgow buildings even in Stirling. Many local people thought of the children who had gone back to their parents—some of them were killed.

Members of the Scouts, Girl Guides and the Boys' Brigade volunteered to help if Stirling was bombed—they wanted to wear uniform all the time so that they would be easily recognised if an emergency happened.

In fact, Stirling was only bombed once. On Saturday 20th July 1940 a German plane dropped two bombs on the town at about 2 o'clock at night. It was being chased away from Glasgow and probably just dumped its unused bombs to get away faster. One bomb fell in a field and caused no damage, but the other destroyed the King's Park FC football ground at Forthbank. (In fact that bomb ended the King's Park club, which is why Stirling Albion was founded in 1945 when the war was over). Some houses across the road from the stadium were damaged and three people were taken to hospital with injuries. The blast from the two bombs was felt all over Stirling—one boy who lived near the castle was knocked right out of bed by it!

Just as in the First World War, many buildings were converted to wartime uses. For example, Allan's School became a recruiting office, Annfield House was used as a medical supply depot, and St Mary's School in the Raploch was even used as a prisoner-of-war camp—German prisoners were used to help build some of the houses in the Cornton area.

One big change to Bridge of Allan was the arrival of many Polish soldiers. When the Germans captured Poland in 1939 thousands of Poles escaped and came to Britain to carry on the fight. Eventually they were sent to Scotland for war training—for a time almost every house in Bridge of Allan was used as a billet for Polish soldiers. Their language, uniforms and manners were very different but they were very polite and people liked them. Local girls thought they were very handsome in their smart uniforms.

During the war many things were in short supply. In 1940 ration books were introduced and food was restricted—eggs, meat, cheese, butter, tea, and anything with sugar in it, like jam or sweets for example. By 1941 clothing was rationed. You got 66 clothing coupons a year—a boy's shirt needed six coupons and a girl's skirt was five. In August 1942 the *Stirling Journal* told people to use no more than five inches of bath water, to save coal in heating

more water. By 1942 milk was in short supply and you got only two pints a week, though children and pregnant mothers got more. Petrol was rationed and most ordinary people couldn't get any. In 1945 coal was added to the list of rationed goods. Life was difficult, but people managed to get by.

In May 1945 Stirling celebrated the defeat of Germany. It was not the end of the war because Japan was still fighting, but the blackout was ended and the lights came back on, which cheered everyone up. Some people lit bonfires in the streets and danced and cheered. The black boy fountain, which had been switched off during the war, was started up again.

The same thing happened when Japan was finally beaten in August 1945. According to the *Stirling Journal*, people rushed into the streets ringing bells, letting off fireworks, lighting bonfires, singing and dancing long into the night. It was quite a celebration.

Boy Scouts, Boys' Brigade, Girl Guides and Army Cadets.

THEY DID MANY **USEFUL** JOBS IN STIRLING DURING THE SECOND WORLD WAR.

Chapter 37

Changing Leisure Time in Stirling

It's been more than 50 years since the end of the Second World War. Compared to the long history of Stirling, fifty years is very little, but an amazing amount of change has happened in that quite short time. This chapter is about one of these great changes—how we spend our leisure time.

Fifty years ago electronic entertainments did not exist—no-one had computers or Game-boys and even TV was just getting started. People had other forms of entertainment. Because there were far fewer cars, children usually played in the streets—boys sometimes played marbles but usually football, often with a tennis ball or even just a tin can if they couldn't afford a ball. The goals were often just two jackets laid on the ground. No-one wore expensive team strips in those days—they just played in their ordinary school clothes. Girls enjoyed skipping—they made up lots of rhymes which they chanted as they skipped over the turning rope. If you think that sounds really *boring* compared to the excitement of electronic games today, just remember one thing—children were probably much fitter in those days than they are today!

Children also read much more than they do today, especially comics like the Beano, the Dandy or the Hotspur. They used to read them during the evenings, or at night in bed, because there was no TV. Can you imagine life without TV? What would you *do* with all that time?

Did you know that during the Second World War there were *four* cinemas in Stirling? At that time most people went to the pictures at least once a week—the film usually ran for three nights, so you could see two different movies each week. Maybe you go sometimes to the Allanpark (which opened in 1938), but in those days you could also have watched films at the Picture House in Orchard Place, the Queens at the top of Queen Street or the Regal in Maxwell Place—*and* there was also the Regent cinema in Bannockburn! Fifty years ago it cost around 3p downstairs and 5p or 6p in the balcony! By 1970 prices at the Allanpark were up to 30p downstairs and 37p upstairs (though children and old folks got in for half price). Perhaps that sounds very cheap but remember that, according to an article in the *Stirling Observer* for 21st July 1970, a child's typical pocket money that year was about 15-20p.

Why does only one cinema survive nowadays? The answer in simple—the invention of TV. Many people bought their first set because of the coronation of Queen Elizabeth in 1953, which was shown on TV. At that time, however, televisions were *very* expensive and many people watched someone else's! By the 1960s televisions were no longer high-priced luxuries—most people had one. The more they stayed in to watch each night, the more cinemas struggled to keep going—even though colour television did not begin until 1968, and there were only two channels—BBC and ITV. To begin with they even had a break in programmes at teatime so that school children could do their homework!

What do you do on a Saturday nowadays? Fifty years ago it's quite likely that boys would go with their fathers to watch football somewhere. Just as today, Rangers and Celtic were the main teams, but there was still a chance for other teams to have success—the Scottish Cup was won by Falkirk in 1957, by Clyde in 1958 and by St Mirren in 1959, for example. Stirling's greatest ever footballer was Billy Bremner, who was a pupil at St Modan's High School before eventually captaining Leeds United during their glory days, and then captaining Scotland in the 1970s.

Stirling Albion was founded in 1945, when the Second World War ended. Do you know how the team got its name? The club was founded by Mr Tom Ferguson, a local coal merchant—he used Albion lorries (a popular make of trucks in those days) for his business and just liked the name! It's strange to think that the team is named after a brand of lorry!

To begin with the team played at Annfield Park, opposite the police headquarters on St Ninians Road. The ground was supposed to have a crowd

60

capacity of 19,400, but the all-time record was 28,600 for a Scottish Cup match against Celtic in 1959. Remember that in those days people stood on the terracing, so they just squeezed up to get more in— the present seated stadium at Forthbank has a crowd capacity of just over 3000. The team's biggest win was in the 1984 Scottish Cup when they beat Selkirk 20-0. Their biggest defeat was 9-0 against Dundee United in a 1968 league match. The closest the club came to big-time success was when they reached the semi-final of the Scottish League Cup in 1961. They played Hearts in front of 26,000 at neutral Easter Road, Edinburgh, but lost 2-1 after extra time.

The local rugby club has also brought success to the town. In 1970 Stirling County moved to its present ground at Bridgehaugh—a change which saw the start of its best run of success so far. From 1976 onwards the team won promotion every year, climbing from division 7 to division 2. They eventually made the first division in 1989 and in season 1994-95 they won the national first division championship. The following year they came first again, only to lose the championship to Melrose on points difference. The club has also produced several outstanding Scottish internationalists—the greatest is perhaps former Wallace High School pupil Kenny Logan, with more than 40 caps for his country.

Although football and rugby perhaps dominate local sports, there are many more which thrive in the area. Stirling County Cricket Club were Scottish champions in 1952 and 1985, and have produced several international players. Pony trotting is very popular at the Corbiewood Stadium, and the swimming club has also produced several champions over the years. Bowling, ten-pin bowling, squash, tennis, golf, skating, curling, table-tennis, gymnastics, snooker and many other sports have grown tremendously in the past fifty years. Quite a change from playing football with a tin can in the street, or skipping with an old rope in the playground!

Libraries are for leisure as well as learning.

Chapter 38

So much Change in One Lifetime

Ask any older person and they will agree—the past 50 years have changed Stirling almost out of recognition. Chapter 37 told you how there used to be four cinemas, and how children played football in the streets, but these are just the tip of a huge iceberg. Stirling has changed *much* more than that. Can you imagine the town before Chinese food or burgers? When cattle and sheep were still herded to market in Wallace Street? When *no-one* had a pocket calculator, or a video, or a walkman, or a microwave? When the trains were still steam-powered and soldiers still lived in Stirling Castle? All these things have changed in just one lifetime.

One of the greatest changes has been the amount of traffic in the town. In the past fifty years car ownership has grown a lot. Now almost everyone has a car and far fewer people use buses or bikes. But there has been a price to pay—in traffic jams, parking restrictions, pollution and noise. Streets are very busy now, and children don't play there any more—it's too dangerous.

Of course Stirling Council has tried to solve the traffic problem. The 'by-pass' road which goes past the bus and railway stations was opened in 1970. This took away some of the traffic which used to go through the centre of the town by Murray Place and Wallace Street. In 1973 the M9 motorway was opened so that through-traffic did not need to go near Stirling at all. But can you *imagine* what it would be like if all these cars and buses and trucks still came through the town and wanted to cross the bridge? Instead, the town centre is a bit quieter—some parts are even pedestrianised and cars are not allowed there at all.

The town has also grown a lot in size. Bannockburn, Cambusbarron, Bridge of Allan and Cambuskenneth used to be quite separate villages but now they are gradually being swallowed up as Stirling spreads wider and wider. In the 1950s the Cornton area was built, followed by the Cultenhove and Torbrex areas in the 1970s, the Braehead area in the 1980s and the Wallace Park district during the 1990s. Bannockburn, Fallin, Plean and Bridge of Allan have also doubled in size during the last fifty years. When you remember that the Victorians were really the first to build outside the old town walls, that's quite an amazing spread!

Shopping has also changed completely. Fifty years ago people still had to go from shop to shop around the town centre—Woolworth's and the Co-op were the only superstores in Stirling. Today the small shops in Stirling town centre are struggling to compete against the Thistle and Marches shopping centres, and superstores like Tesco's and Safeway. Why get cold and wet trailing round the town when you can buy everything under one roof? You can keep dry and warm, have a bite to eat, and the prices are likely to be lower. Are small shops finished?

Prices have also changed, mostly because the value of money is different now. In 1970 you could buy a t-shirt for 35p, a ladies' dress for £1.50, and a pair of ladies' shoes for £1.45p. Trainers (called 'tennis shoes' in those days) cost around 75p. In the food shops a packet of chocolate biscuits cost 8p, a packet of tea was 13p, a tin of soup was 9p, baked beans cost 6p and a jar of Nescafe was 41p. A typical magazine cost 15p, while a single record cost 35p—CDs and minidisks didn't exist at all. In 1970 Supertramp and Hawkwind, which were quite famous rock bands at that time, played a concert at the Albert Hall—tickets cost 50p!

For your parents, TV rental was 44p per week and a new fridge cost around £50. A second-hand Ford Escort cost about £650, and you could buy a new six-roomed house for £6,950. You might think that these prices are low, but you must compare them with what people earned. A typical typist only earned about £500—£700 a year. A policeman was paid just £1025 a year. The janitor at Fallin Primary School was paid only £16.90 a week, which works out at less than £900 a year. If you had a paper round in those days, you would only have earned about 8p a week! So that 50p ticket for the rock concert would actually have been quite expensive.

Even the coins you use have changed. Up to 1971 people used 'old' money—pounds, shillings and pence. There were 12 pence in one shilling and 20 shillings in one pound—that's 240 pennies in one pound, and each penny was bigger than a modern 5p coin. All this changed in 1971 when 'decimalisation' began. That's when the money which we use today came into use. Can you imagine the confusion which people felt when they saw prices in the 'new' money?

Schools have also changed a lot. In the past every pupil in Primary 7 had to sit the '11+' exam. The ones who were clever and passed went to Stirling High School, where they eventually sat their 'O Grade' and 'Higher' exams. The ones who didn't do so well went to the 'junior secondary' at Riverside, where they trained for practical jobs like hairdressing or motor mechanics—in those days they could leave school aged 15. All this changed in 1971 when 'comprehensive education' began. From then on all pupils went to the same kind of mixed-ability school. Wallace High School, which opened that year, was therefore a purpose-built comprehensive school and Riverside changed to a primary school, but Stirling High School and St Modan's also changed to accept the new system. Many teachers didn't like it. The mixture of all abilities was difficult for some of them to get used to, but in the end it all settled down.

One of the biggest changes to hit Stirling was the opening of the university in 1967. Nowadays we take the sight of students for granted—even those dressed in the clothes of foreign countries are a perfectly normal part of Stirling life. It's hard to imagine what it was like when the students first arrived—for example, the police were not used to seeing anybody out after about 11 o'clock at night, so students heading home from late night parties were often stopped! People were not used to seeing young folk in trendy clothes, or crowding into pubs, or even just walking around with their books or guitars. How times have changed! Now we go to the MacRobert Theatre, or take a walk through the university grounds to feed the ducks, or play on the golf course, surrounded by people from all over the world.

What a change from the Stirling our ancestors knew!

Changed days in Stirling.

63

The council considering that it was Some time agoe resolved upon to offer his Royal Highness the Duke of Cumberland and his Highness the Prince of Hesse the Complement of the town, and that in order thereto two Burgess Tickets have been made out properly Embelished and Gilded. But it being judged proper that these Tickets should be put and delivered in Boxes made for the purpose, The Council therefore aggreed that a Silver Box, richly made and Gilded be prepared for each of these Tickets and capable to contain them and the Seal, and that the Town's Arms, to witt the wolf on the Craig, be Engraved on each of these Boxes, and all done and Execute in the handsomest manner and with all dispatch.

Willm. Danskin DG.

If you look inside the front cover of this book, you will see an example of a page taken from the old records of Stirling's town council. This is another example. It was written in 1746 soon after the Government army had chased Bonnie Prince Charlie and his Jacobite supporters out of Stirling.

Bonnie Prince Charlie and his army occupied Stirling on the 8th of January 1746, but they did not manage to capture the castle. On the 1st of February they left again because the Government army was getting close. The commander of the Government soldiers was the Duke of Cumberland. Later he caught up with Charlie and defeated his army at the Battle of Culloden. You can read all about it on page 41 of this book.

This extract tells us that Stirling's town council decided to show their gratitude to the Duke of Cumberland, and also the Prince of Hesse, by making them both honorary members of Stirling's population. They did this by presenting them each with a *burgess ticket* contained in specially made, beautifully carved, silver boxes.